NEW
MANAGEMENT
ACCOUNTING

*How Leading-Edge Companies
Use Management Accounting
to Improve Performance*

EDITOR
WILLIAM F. CHRISTOPHER

WITHDRAWN

CRISP PUBLICATIONS

Editor-in-Chief: *William F. Christopher*

Project Editor: *Kay Keppler*

Editor: *Michael Koch*

Cover Design: *Kathleen Barcos*

Cover Production: *Russell Leong Design*

Book Design & Production: *London Road Design*

Printer: *Bawden Printing*

Library of Congress Card Catalog Number 97-68250

ISBN 1-56052-444-8

NEW
MANAGEMENT
ACCOUNTING

How Leading-Edge Companies
Use Management Accounting
to Improve Performance

CONTENTS

INTRODUCTION

There's a revolution going on in management accounting!
Pioneering companies are making management accounting
a new and different information resource for action planning, performance measurement, and decision support.
No longer do the numbers all have dollar signs in front
of them. No longer does decision support rely entirely on
measures quantified in numbers; qualitative measures can
be helpful, too.

In the new management accounting, the measures
continue to be used for performance evaluation, but this
is not their main purpose. More and more the measures
focus on producing results. They help people do the right
things, right. At all levels, measures become the information feedback that informs and empowers people to
accomplish desired results.

This fast-moving revolution is forming from conver-
gence of three innovative streams:

1. Accounting and financial theory, methods, and
   measures. The perspective of finance and accounting is more and more looking behind and beyond
   financial measures to embrace the drivers of good
   financial performance.

2. Economics, and specifically managerial economics—the economics of the profit center business.
   As accounting and finance broaden their focus,

economics while maintaining a broad focus on
the economy, also focuses a perceptive wisdom
on the economics of the firm.

3. The Quality Movement. Total Quality Management (TQM) and the methods and measures of
quality and productivity improvement are changing and improving the way work is done, changing
and improving organization performance.

You will see these three streams at work in the
reports of the leading edge companies whose stories
appear in this book. You will see not prescriptions, but
works in progress. The best in management accounting is
a journey of change and continuing improvement. We can
benchmark with firms like those reporting here, change
and improve our present practices to these standards,
then continue the journey of continuing improvement.

The New Managment Accounting

Vanguard companies, like those reporting in this book,
are finding the measures that make visible all that really
matters, for all those who need and use the information.
Management accounting for these companies is becoming
"world-class performance measurement."

Some of the companies presented in this book report
on measures used by executive management to guide total
company and profit center performance. Some report on
measures that provide people at all levels reliable information for their decisions and actions. At all levels, these are
the key performance measures that will determine what

the financial results will be. Financial measures are included, but more than financials are needed. In each company, profit center and unit, what is needed are their key measures of success.

Much of the revolution in performance measurement concentrates on the important performance areas that drive company success and determine the financial results. These measures tend to group into the key performance areas long recommended by Peter Drucker:

- Productivity and Quality
- Innovation of New Products, Services, Processes
- Market Position/Customer Satisfaction
- Profitability
- Organization Capability and Motivation
- Capital Resource Management
- Community, Government, and Environmental Relationships

Typically, in the past, measures have been designed to show actual in comparison with plan, and variances. In the new management accounting the most useful measures show trends and changes in trends. Trend measures show how we are progressing toward our goals, and signal when changes are needed. Changing from variances to trends can be a significant success builder.

The new management accounting puts the focus squarely on performance. Structures form to accomplish desired goals. Organizations become less hierarchical; jobs and positions less fixed, more fluid. Seeing this trend, in 1997 Acxiom eliminated executive titles. The former executives are now "leaders" and "champions."

The search for better measures has many consequences. Finding the best measures for evaluating performance is one. But a broader and deeper perspective is needed:

- **Broader.** Management needs more than measures for the evaluation of company and subordinates' performance. They need information for their own performance—the information that will help them do what needs to be done at the executive level to accomplish company goals. Measures are needed to perform. In world-class companies every person and every process is a performer, producing an output that is needed to accomplish company goals. Information directs and controls performance. As reported by the companies in this book, measures become performance tools.

- **Deeper.** A family of performance measures is needed not only for senior management, but also for decision-makers at all levels, in all units, to the level of the individual process and work station. For each, the family of performance measures is different; unique for that unit. The measures control and motivate the performance needed from that unit to accomplish its purpose, and contribute to company success. Companies reporting in this book describe how their new management accounting measures align, support and motivate all areas of company operations.

Information System Design

How are all the activities in all parts of the enterprise so conducted that appropriate objectives are established and then in operations are achieved? Managing with the right kind of information feedback going to each group, team, and person can direct this kind of performance in all units.

With this approach, control is not something imposed from a higher level. Instead, control is built into each unit. Once the structure includes the right kind of measures and feedback, as the companies in this book report, control can become self-control and the unit can more or less organize itself and control its performance through information feedback.

Company Vision

A powerful influence for integrating company people and actions toward desired goals is the development and communication of a motivating Company Vision. The simplicity of a good vision statement belies the complexity of its creation. From the process of its creation comes the power of its influence. A vision statement is an attractive word picture of an achievable future. Creating a vision statement requires an understanding of the past up to now, an awareness of the winds of change now perceivable, and a view ahead for the lifetime of the strategy and investment decisions being made today. So a vision statement does not come lightly. It requires input from many; dialog with many. All learn from the process. And when the vision statement is at last created it will be known, and agreed with, by those committed to make it happen. For everyone it says what the company aims for, and can become tomorrow, and onward into the 21st century.

Some vision statements from the past that created an intended future:

- Henry Ford: Build a car everyone can buy

- NASA: Put a man on the moon by the end of the decade

- Disneyland: Create a place for people to find happiness and knowledge

Henry Ford's vision was good for twenty years. NASA's for a decade. Disney's is still going. Visions from time to time may have to be ratcheted forward to find and create new successes.

But when we have a clear vision, the road ahead can be mapped. A first step in mapping will be to make the vision specific through strategy, values, goals, and measures. Just as an airplane has a control panel for directing it to its selected destination, goals and measures become the control panel for piloting the organization to its intended future. And from the company vision, strategy, values, goals, and measures the information feedback system throughout the company can be derived.

The new management accounting described in the company reports in this book can produce the right information at the right place at the right time to create company success.

Useful Steps

Developing and using the New Management Accounting is a journey, not a destination. The measures are a partner in this journey, and a driver of continuing improvement. As the companies in this book report, best practices in management accounting continuously evolve in a journey of continuing improvement. Some useful steps in the journey include:

- **Relating measures at all levels to the company's vision and strategic goals.**   The right management accounting measures can align and integrate all company actions with company strategy and goals, empowering each person, work group and unit to accomplish desired results. The chapters by Honeywell's MICRO SWITCH Division, Acxiom, Alpha Industries, Briggs & Stratton, and Analog Devices provide examples.

- **Total Quality Methods and Management.**   The powerful concepts and methods of Total Quality Management are helping many companies change and improve their performance. For these companies, TQM is providing many of the metrics for the new management accounting. Acxiom, Pitney Bowes,

Honeywell's MICRO SWITCH Division and Analog Devices are examples.

- **Activity Based Costing (ABC) and Activity Based Management (ABM).** When we know what costs are incurred for specific company actions (activities) we can better manage these costs and the creation of customer values. Using ABC and ABM methods, companies can improve their management of costs to profitably satisfy customer expectations. Axiom and Alpha Industries provide examples.

- **Value Added.** Creating values for customers is the basic purpose of all organizations. In management accounting, value added is the measure. Improving work processes to eliminate non-value adding steps sharply reduces waste, reduces costs and improves quality. You will see value added in all these company examples. Alpha Industries' program to find and eliminate non-value adding activities identifies their costs; then improves processes to reduce or eliminate these costs.

- **Economic Value Added (EVA).** Without EVA or similar measures, companies do not recognize the real cost of the capital resources they use, and often over-report their profitability. EVA measures help reduce hidden and often excessive capital costs, improve productivity, and significantly improve profitability. Briggs & Stratton and Acxiom describe their experiences with EVA.

- **Redesigning Work Processes.** Reorganizing the way work is done can significantly reduce cost, increase output and improve productivity and quality. Alpha Industries, Honeywell's MICRO SWITCH Division, Briggs & Stratton, and Analog Devices provide examples.

- **Lean, Agile Manufacturing.** An on-going revolution in manufacturing technology and methods has created new standards for world-class competitiveness. The best of these new technologies and methods combine in what we now refer to as "lean, agile manufacturing." The new management accounting provides the measures, and links manufacturing with product and process design on the front end and marketing on the output end to control costs and satisfy customer expectations. Chapter 3, "Manufacturing Cost Management," describes methods.

- **Target Costing.** World-class companies plan and design to achieve needed costs, Target costing is up-front cost planning, rather than after-the-fact cost measurement. Target costing creates the cost structure needed to succeed in today's competitive markets. For information on target costing, see Chapter 4, "Manufacturing Cost Management."

- **Training and Development.** The new methods and measures have to be learned and used throughout the organization. Effective training and development programs are an essential part of the new management accounting. Acxiom, Pitney Bowes, and Briggs & Stratton provide some examples.

- **Incentive Compensation.** The measures of the new management accounting provide an objective, rational basis for incentive compensation plans. Acxiom and Briggs & Stratton describe their experiences.

I.

THE NEW MANAGEMENT ACCOUNTING SYSTEM AT HONEYWELL'S MICRO SWITCH DIVISION

RICHARD D. JONES
*Director of Quality, Environment,
and Supply Management*

EVERY YEAR THOUSANDS of corporations spend hundreds of thousands of hours creating and preparing long-term business plans. Difficult decisions are made, new issues are raised, blood pressures rise, markets fall, and probing questions are asked. Through all of the planning and debating, however, one notion always seems to hold true: the job ahead is really the tough part—communicating, aligning, executing, and measurement. Yet, every year many senior managers either do not realize their plans are being poorly executed or they reach a false conclusion that the problem must lie in the pages of last year's plan.

Honeywell Inc. is a publicly owned, global enterprise with operations in 95 countries and annual revenues of

$7.3 billion. Honeywell's MICRO SWITCH Division
has enjoyed incredible success using new approaches in
management accounting to administer the tough parts of
strategic planning. MICRO SWITCH management has
discovered a way to combine its world-class business culture with its unique goal alignment system to drive strategic planning all the way to the factory floor. The process
begins by asking, "How do we create value?"

Value Creation

All organizations exist to create value. At Honeywell's
MICRO SWITCH Division, this process is defined and
guided by senior management. The process (see Figure
1-1) begins with *leadership*. Detailed training and workshop
experiences in leadership are required for all managers,
supervisors and individual team leaders. Why? Because
we believe that leadership ignites the value creation
process and a *world-class workforce*.

This workforce uses a knowledge-based approach
to identify the *best practices* needed to create and manage
business processes. These business processes are focused
on determining the needs and wants of customers, both
short- and long-term. When their needs and wants are
met, customers express their delight. One of the measures
of *customer delight* is the customer's commitment to growing
the MICRO SWITCH business. Customer commitment
helps build a stronger, more *robust business,* and this strong
performance leads to selected reinvestments and a hand-
some return to the stakeholders of the business.

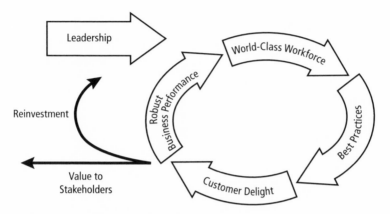

Figure 1-1. Value creation process

Honeywell's MICRO SWITCH Division creates value for four primary stakeholders:

1. Customers: *Customer value* means instant access to highly reliable, defect-free products and services that enhance their competitiveness.

2. Employees: *Personal value* is personal growth, recognition and rewards, and quality of worklife for all.

3. Shareholders: *Shareholder value* is generating ever-increasing returns for all investors with the proper balance between short-term results and long-term growth.

4. Community members: *Community value* means sharing our capabilities and resources for the betterment of the communities in which we live and work.

The value creation process is the foundation around which we communicate and align our strategic initiatives. It is understood by all employees and provides them with a fundamental template to organize and communicate local action plans that support organizational strategies.

The system is comprised of four major processes:

- Strategic planning

- The development of local control boards to align long-term strategic actions

- The development of local goals and measures boards to focus day-to-day activities toward strategy-supporting actions

- The use of a cross-functional total quality management council to drive continuous improvement across the business

Strategic Planning

Strategic planning begins at the highest level of the business, the enterprise level, and cascades down throughout the organization. It is an inclusive process that involves more than 200 managers and team leaders. Once enterprise-level planning is complete, the results of this activity are shared with all functional and support groups. These groups then work interdependently to create support plans and strategies that feed back to the enterprise.

At the enterprise level, the strategic planning process involves five sequential steps:

1. A review of the business foundations

2. A situation analysis

3. A current conditions analysis

4. The development of issues

5. The creation of strategic initiatives

The *review of business foundations* involves an open analysis of the vision, values, mission, and core competencies of the organization. During this step, the leaders of the organization will challenge themselves on the clarity of their vision. They will debate whether their behavior is aligned with the stated values of the organization; they will question if their mission continues to be an appropriate one; and they will challenge one another on the validity of the organization's stated core competencies. Although there may be only minor changes in the basic business foundations from one year to the next, all are thoroughly examined and debated at length to ensure that the business foundation is indeed a firm one.

Once the basic business foundation has been reaffirmed, the *situation analysis* identifies the internal and external issues that have the potential to influence significantly the competitiveness of the company. Issues examined include stakeholder constraints, competitive analyses, emerging technologies, global environmental scans, and human resources. A selection process is used to identify the issues that will have the greatest impact on the company's ability to succeed. These issues are then debated and action statements are created to address each of them.

Where possible, elements of the action statements are combined and the resulting, higher-level action statements are rewritten as enterprise-level strategy statements. The highest priority strategy statements are selected from this list and become *strategic initiatives*. To insure linkage, the strategic initiatives are then examined with respect to the business foundations, situation analysis, and current conditions.

The work product from the enterprise-level strategic planning process is then shared with business teams, functional groups, and support organizations. The planning process cascades throughout the organization and is aligned through two primary mechanisms: local control boards and local goals and measures boards.

Local Control Boards

The local control board (LCB) is the primary tool for communicating and managing the operational priorities of each department and work unit as they relate to long-term goals of the *enterprise-level strategic plan* (ELSP). Since the LCB will be directly linked to the strategic plan, the choices and strategic alternatives reflect a longer-term perspective. The common format of the LCB and its content allows it to play a key role in communicating support group and enterprise-level strategies. When properly deployed, local control boards will:

- Display the *key alternatives* that the department or work unit has determined will best support the ELSP.

- Depict the *desired state* and the *current state* of the department with respect to these key alternatives. (Since the LCB identifies both states, the organization can clearly see the gap between how the unit is performing–the current state–and the performance level needed to support the ELSP–the desired state.)

- Identify the *principal tactics* that the work unit has determined will drive it from its present performance level to the desired state. These tactics also become the objectives of the department or work unit manager.

The success of the LCB lies in its simplicity, format, and content. The structure of the boards is visually very clean and simple to understand. Information is organized into four major categories (or columns), which in turn are divided into a series of subcategories. Since the ultimate goal of strategic planning is to sustain the long-term value creation process of the business, the four major categories of the LCB are the four primary elements of the MICRO SWITCH value creation process: *World-Class Workforce, Best Practices, Customer Delight,* and *Robust Business* (see Figure 1-2). Employees can easily interpret the strategic support initiatives of other departments since the format is standardized across the business. This helps make the LCB a powerful tool in aligning the organization's long-term strategic initiatives.

Each of the subcategories represents strategic alternatives–that is, the choices that the work unit or department has made to support the enterprise-level strategic plan. In

7

The Company's Value Creation Process			1997 CONTROL BOARD Purchasing Department						The Company's Enterprise-Level Strategic Initiatives		
World-Class Workforce			Best Practices			Customer Delight			Robust Business		
Selection & Placement	Reward & Recognition	Training & Education	Partnering Process	Supplier Selection	Quality Control	On-Time Delivery	Invoice Accuracy	Supplier Lead-Time	Total Cost Savings	Inventory Turns	Active Suppliers

Figure 1-2.   The local control board is the primary tool for communicating and managing operational priorities

the example shown in Figure 1-3, the strategic alternative selected to help achieve a world-class workforce is selection and placement. One must assume that the work group or department in this example has evidence that indicates improvements must be made in this area to support the ELSP people issue: "How do we attract and retain the engineering talent required to . . . ?" Once the strategic alternative has been defined, the team determines the most favorable condition with respect to this alternative. This condition is summarized in three to five words and placed at the top of the subcategory.

Next, the team determines the least favorable point and summarizes it at the bottom of the column.

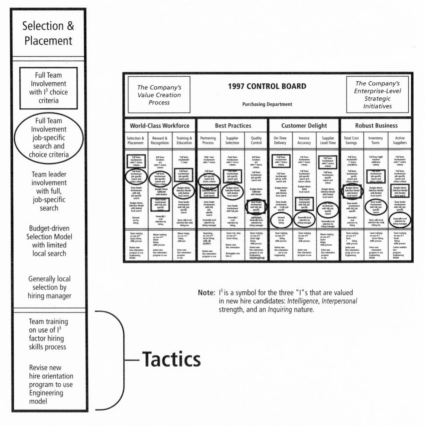

Selection & Placement
Full Team Involvement with I³ choice criteria
Full Team Involvement job-specific search and choice criteria
Team leader involvement with full, job-specific search
Budget-driven Selection Model with limited local search
Generally local selection by hiring manager
Team training on use of I³ factor hiring skills process
Revise new hire orientation program to use Engineering model

Note: I³ is a symbol for the three "I"s that are valued in new hire candidates: *Intelligence, Interpersonal* strength, and an *Inquiring* nature.

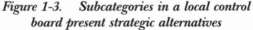

—Tactics

*Figure 1-3.   Subcategories in a local control
board present strategic alternatives*

Intermediate positions are determined to complete the continuum. When the column has been completed, the group will use internal customers, benchmark data, and existing measurements to determine their *current position* along the continuum. This "general" position is marked with a circle. Employees will use similar input as well as data from the ELSP to determine where they *should be* and this will be identified using a square or rectangle. The difference between the two points represents a gap that the group must develop *tactics* to close. In some cases, gaps may not exist and, consequently, no improvement tactics are required.

The tactics for the LCB are typically displayed at the bottom of each respective column. In some cases, groups may choose to display their gap-closing tactics on a separate board posted adjacent to the LCB. In any case, the tactics become part of the quarterly objectives of the supervisor or team leader and are visibly displayed to communicate strategic priorities.

Deploying LCBs completes the long-term execution branch of the strategic planning process, as shown in Figure 1-4.

Local Goals and Measures Boards

The local goals and measures board (LGMB) is the communicative vehicle that each department and work unit uses to quantitatively report its short-term performance in areas that closely link to ELSP strategic initiatives. LGMBs are deployed to address the short-term execution branch of the system, as shown in Figure 1-5. As with the LCB, the common format of the LGMB and its personalized content make it a powerful tool in aligning goals and building cross-functional support. When properly deployed, LGMBs:

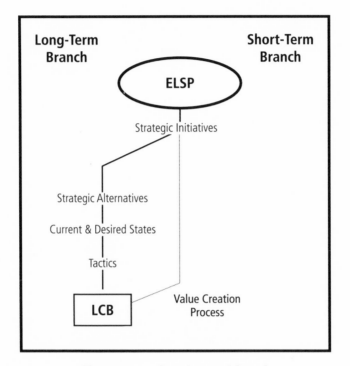

Figure 1-4. Local control boards
complete the long-term execution branch
of the strategic planning process

- Display the organization's *key business drivers*. Derived
  from the strategic initiatives, key business drivers are
  the unique items that the organization must do well
  for its strategies to succeed. Key business drivers are
  sufficiently specific that effective companywide understanding and continual action can be drawn from
  them.

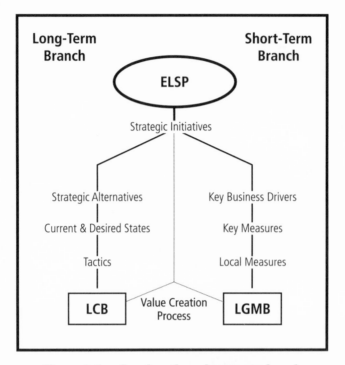

*Figure 1-5.   Local goals and measures boards
complete the short-term execution branch
of the strategic planning process*

- Depict the organization's performance against its *key
  measures.* Key measures represent the numerical information that quantifies the critical dimensions of key
  business drivers. (Each key business driver will have
  at least one key measure.) To gain sustainable goal
  alignment, the metrics must be common and easily
  understood by most employees. Consequently,
  simplicity is a principal characteristic of a good key

measure. For example, an important key business driver continues to be *responsiveness*. Having employees deliver results through agile and efficient processes is critical to competing successfully. In our case, responsiveness must be measured in two ways: (1) the responsiveness needed to *earn* new business and (2) the responsiveness needed to *keep* existing business. Hence, we have two key measures for responsiveness: new product time-to-market and current product on-time-delivery-to-customer request.

- Display the work unit or department's performance against its *local goals and measures*. Local goals and measures are either directly linked to the organization's key measures or they are metrics that embody the spirit of the key measure. Local goals and measures, like key measures, are updated and reported every month.

The LGMB is displayed adjacent to the LCB. Each department or work unit follows the same general design for layout and size. Once again, a common design assists employee interpretation, fosters unity, and strengthens alignment. As employees move from one department to another, they can quickly identify the critical performance metrics of the new area. The key measures, structural format, and language remain unchanged; only the work unit metrics will be different. The LGMB displays both the key measures for the organization and the local measures for the work unit or department.

We spend considerable time each year explaining the strategic initiatives, the key business drivers, and the

associated key measures. The communication plan typically includes management presentations, monthly video-
tapes, departmental posters and banners, and hard-copy
training materials. Since high-level business strategy does
not dramatically shift from one year to the next, many
of the key business drivers and key measures remain
unchanged for three to five years.

Figure 1-6 shows the key business drivers, key
measures, and local measures used in the purchasing
organization in 1995.

In some cases, a department or work unit will provide direct input into a key measure. An example might
be a company that uses internal product quality as a key
measure. The PPM quality data from each of the company's production lines will be combined to yield the
aggregate quality measure. Yet, many departments will
find that they do not have local measures that are aggre-
gated into this particular key measure. In these cases, a
related measure is adopted by the department.

For example, if the local department is the mail
room, the employees may have difficulty aligning with a
key measure such as internal product quality or customer
responsiveness. An *aligned* group of mail room employees
will recognize that they have internal customers throughout the entire company. With this in mind, they might
select daily package delivery as a measure to embody the
spirit of customer responsiveness and destination accuracy
as their quality measure. When multiplied throughout the
entire company, the overall result is that all employees will
directly contribute to or embody the spirit of key measures and display similar behaviors toward their internal
customers.

14

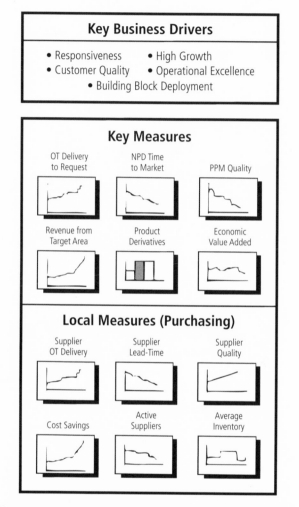

Figure 1-6.   Honeywell's MICRO SWITCH Division's key business drivers, key measures, and local measures

As each department or work unit deploys the improvement tactics outlined in their LCBs, their local goals and measures will reflect a favorable trend. As these trends are sustained across the organization, the key measures will respond favorably and the longer-term LCB gaps will close.

The Total Quality Management Council

The process for communicating strategy and aligning goals and measures is the responsibility of senior management. The management team has created a cross-functional total quality management council (TQMC) to measure and continuously improve its internal business processes. There is a *Category Team* for each of the seven categories of the Malcolm Baldrige National Quality Award:

- Leadership
- Strategic Planning
- Customer and Market Focus
- Information and Analysis
- Human Resource Development and Management
- Process Management
- Business Results

Each of the category teams is comprised of 5 to 12 employees from across the business. The leaders of each of the category teams form the *Total Quality Management Council.*

The category teams covering Strategic Planning and Business Results are chartered to continuously improve the goals and measures system throughout the company.

II.

ACXIOM'S QUALITY JOURNEY

RODGER S. KLINE
Corporate Office, Operations

ACXIOM CORPORATION BEGAN as a data processing services company in 1969. It has grown through several stages of development to become almost a $500 million company, with plans to become a multibillion dollar corporation. As in any business, major critical decisions had to be made to keep the company on its growth track and to navigate around obstacles such as changes in the business environment.

From my perspective, two critical decision points along Acxiom's development path stand out from all of the others:

1.   Development of a specialized niche. In its early years, Acxiom was a full-service direct marketing company that also provided all forms of data processing services, including supporting manufacturers, construction companies, accountants, and so on. In the mid-1970s we faced an economic downturn and the loss of our largest, most profitable customer. The end result of this

critical decision point was that we made a decision to focus all of our energies and talents on a narrow area of specialty so that we could develop world-class solutions in our niche. We chose information processing services supporting large-scale, commercial, direct mail advertising as our specialty niche area. We initiated a plan to phase out our other lines of business and to develop state-of-the-art software and solutions in our chosen niche. This specialization led Acxiom on a course to become a recognized leader in its field in the United States and Europe. Since initiating this strategy, we have experienced a compound growth rate of more than 30%, as shown in Figure 2-1.

2. Growth beyond $100 million in revenue. By 1990, Acxiom had passed several milestones in its development, including going public in 1983 with revenues of approximately $7.5 million. We were also recognized by the direct marketing industry for building the first marketing database in the industry. We continued to add new customer relationships that continued our growth and were looking to reach $100 million in revenues.

Charles Morgan, Acxiom's chairman, recognized that change would be required to facilitate the company's continued growth. In 1990, he began our quality initiative. Two years later, we experienced our first downturn in

Revenue
For the Years Ended March 31

Millions

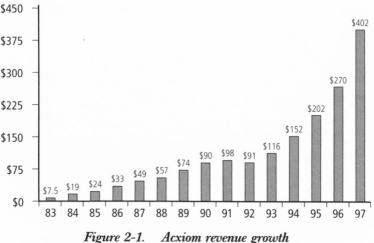

Figure 2-1.   Acxiom revenue growth

revenues since the mid-1970s. This was primarily due
to external economic factors—including the Gulf War,
a business downturn in the United Kingdom, and a 30%
postal rate increase for business mailers.

At this critical decision point, we accelerated the
development of our new quality-based business culture.
We reorganized our business, flattened our management
structure, and eliminated titles.

The development of this quality-based business culture which led to *activity-based costing and management* and the
adoption of *economic value added* as our primary financial

measure is the subject of this case study. The successful development of these initiatives led us through these business challenges and facilitated Acxiom's continued success in our goal to become a multibillion dollar corporation.

Quality Initiative

The quality initiative at Acxiom began with benchmarking visits to companies such as Milliken, Xerox, and Hewlett Packard. It was through these visits that Acxiom first became informed about what was going on with the quality movement in American business. All senior Acxiom executives were encouraged to make at least one benchmarking visit to a company that had experienced success with a quality program.

Once that was completed, Charles attended a one-week course at the Crosby Quality College in Winter Park, Florida. After returning from Crosby College, Charles was a dedicated disciple of the quality movement and the champion for Acxiom's quality initiative. Mark Bailey, an experienced total quality management (TQM) facilitator/coordinator, was hired and a project team was formed to develop Acxiom's quality initiative.

The Acxiom quality team was formed with representatives from across the company who had participated in at least one TQM benchmarking visit. The team designed an Acxiom customized quality plan as well as a three-day education course for training Acxiom's associates. Acxiom adopted the Best-of-Breed practices from all of the companies benchmarked as well as the appropriate portions of the Crosby College quality course. We named our plan

Race for Excellence Actions

Figure 2-2.   Acxiom's race for excellence

Acxiom's race for excellence (RFE) and launched a one-year training program, modeled after Xerox's top-down education process, to train all Acxiom associates (see Figure 2-2).

After eight years in the quality journey, we continue to refine our quality initiatives with the goal of continuously improving Acxiom's business processes (see Figure 2-3).

In retrospect, it took two to three years of the journey for the average Acxiom associate to get a clear understanding of what quality is all about. To this day, we continue to see increases in beneficial results.

Acxiom's RFE spawned the search for a new measurement system. This initially resulted in an *activity-based*

1. Leadership-Based Culture
   - Eliminate manager and director titles   Year 1
   - Eliminate technical and professional titles   Year 3
   - Eliminate all titles from business cards   Year 4
   - Eliminate executive titles (V.P., E.V.P., etc.)   Year 7
   - Eliminate the term executive from business culture   Year 8
   - Eliminate corporate officer titles   Year 8

2. Flatten Organizational Structure
   - Business unit structure   Year 2
   - Three levels of management   Year 3
   - Business unit franchise agreement developed   Year 4
   - Eliminate organizational chart   Year 4
   - Replace with leadership alignment chart   Year 8

3. High-Performance Work Teams/Professional Services Work Model
   - Project orientation   Year 1
   - No permanently assigned project managers   Year 3
   - Peer-to-peer reviews   Year 4
   - Project reviews   Year 5

4. Training
   - RFE initial training   Year 2
   - FADE training (Focus, Analyze, Develop, Execute)   Year 2
   - Teaming training   Year 3
   - RFEII training   Year 3
   - ABM training   Year 4
   - EVA training   Year 6
   - Quest for Excellence—additional training   Year 8

Figure 2-3. Actions supporting quality initiatives

costing project, and later in adopting *activity-based management* and *economic value added* as our primary cost collection and measurement systems at Acxiom. These systems coordinate well with our quality-based business culture. As our business culture developed, RFE became RFE II, which became just the Acxiom business culture, or the way we do business.

Activity-Based Management

After the initial training in 1991, Charles Morgan established an RFE steering committee. This steering committee assigned owners to the parts of the RFE, including customer satisfaction, associate satisfaction, profitability, financial measurements, and so on.

Ownership of developing a new measurement system to support the quality-based business culture was given to Bob Bloom, Chief Financial Officer. After evaluating several options, Bob began an *activity-based costing* study at Acxiom. He also engaged a consulting firm associated with the American Productivity and Quality Center in Houston, Texas, to complete Phase I of an *activity-based costing* project at Acxiom. This project included the identification of Acxiom business processes and activities that associates spent their time on to support our customers. It led to a new way of measuring our costs and allocating them for profit analysis by project, customer, and Acxiom product and service lines.

An activity-based costing project team was formed to work with the consultants to complete this study. At the end of the study, the entire executive team was presented with the result as part of a training session on *activity-based costing*. At the completion of that session, we adopted a more comprehensive activity-based methodology, termed activity-based management (ABM) and made it Acxiom's official measurement and cost collection system to support our quality initiative.

By the end of our Phase I ABM project, we had defined approximately 200 activities and collected cost information tied to those activities and their associated business processes. We again launched a training initiative–this time to train our associates on *activity-based management* and how to use the new measures to generate improved business results. Part of this training course included how to identify the business processes for each team and business unit and then how to flowchart these business processes to identify all of the steps involved in accomplishing the business process. This business process mapping became a powerful tool at Acxiom. Over the next several years, we tied parts of our incentive system to completing these business process maps. The goal was to identify opportunities to streamline the processes and to eliminate unnecessary and redundant steps, thus dramatically improving the cycle times.

Figure 2-4 shows an example of the kinds of improvements we began experiencing all across the company using this technique. The business process mapping and the improvements it generated, in my judgment, contributed more than enough benefits to justify the costs of the entire quality initiative.

In Figure 2-4, the decision to outsource part of the press release distribution process provided the following results:

- Significant reduction of hours by Acxiom investor relations

Press Release Distribution
Process Improvement

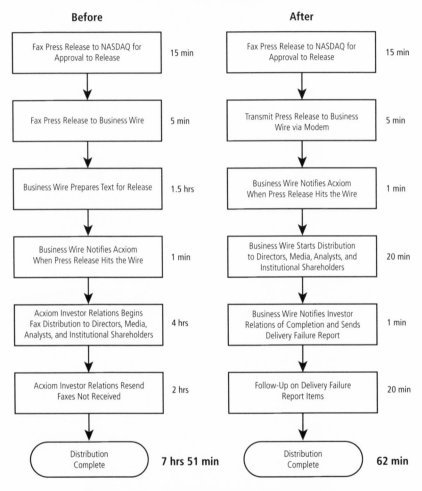

Figure 2-4. *Improvements in the press release distribution through business process mapping*

- Timely delivery of press release information
- Reduction in office equipment

Over the years, we have continued to refine and improve our ABM measures at Acxiom. We have added an ABM-relational database to house our cost and profitability data. We have provided access to this database for all business units so that they can continue to identify and implement improved efficiencies and understand through their own custom analysis the profitability of their customer projects. These ABM initiatives and their continued refinement led Acxiom to a new way of viewing our financial results. This progress was another step in our quality journey and was a natural precursor to the adoption of *economic value added* (EVA) as our primary measure of financial results.

Economic Value Added

In late 1992, Acxiom financial analyst Jeff Pascoe, Bob Bloom, and I attended Stern Stewart's EVA Conference in New York. By the end of the conference, we were all won over to the EVA concept.

After returning from the conference, our top priority was to get our chairman to attend the Stern Stewart conference so that we could get his support to move forward with implementing EVA at Acxiom. Charles Morgan attended a Stern Stewart EVA conference in early 1993.

What attracted us all to the EVA concept was that:

- EVA allowed for the same kinds of adjustments to traditional GAAP accounting that we were already making to set our financial targets for incentive pay systems.

- EVA financial measures included an accountability for capital expenditures (i.e., the cost of capital deployed in the business).

- EVA as a financial measure provided the benefit of standardizing on one balanced financial measure rather than multiple traditional measures (i.e., earnings, profit margin, return on equity, return on assets, and so on).

EVA gave us an opportunity to fill in the missing gaps in our financial measures. It gave us a way to build accountability for capital expenditures into a balanced measure for our operating units. And, for the first time, it included operating unit accountability for balance sheet items. Balance sheet items that factor into EVA include a cost of capital charge to the operating units for:

- Accounts receivable

- Computer hardware and software to support their customers

- Buildings, personal computers, telephone equipment, and the like needed to support each associate

Because of these benefits, we decided to move forward immediately with EVA implementation.

We began with education for our executives, continued with training for all associates, and then added tie-ins to incentive compensation. We progressed to using an EVA analysis as primary input to the decision when evaluating all major capital expenditures and acquisition/ divestiture opportunities. Today we also have an EVA pricing model that runs on the PC and helps ensure that positive EVA is generated for each new customer project that we price. Even our salespeople have EVA models on their laptop computers to assist in understanding the costs and pricing of new customer projects that they are negotiating.

At this point, just about everyone in the company understands that if we cannot generate positive economic value for Acxiom from a proposed project, we probably shouldn't invest our critical resources in doing the project at all. This is a dramatic improvement in perspective.

To gain commitment to the EVA concept, we decided to tie incentive compensation to economic value attained rather than revenues and direct profits which we had previously used as our attainment measurement. One of the goals of our incentive compensation systems is to align leaders' and associates' interests with shareholders' interests. We have been careful to ensure that we build incentives so that what is good for associates is also good for shareholders. We began slowly by allocating a portion of the attainment goal to improvement in EVA. We progressed over five years to base more of the incentive on EVA. We now base 100% of the attainment objectives for all Acxiom incentive systems, other than sales commissions, on EVA attainment. This includes all leadership and associate incentive systems. We are even beginning to include EVA goals in our individual sales commissions plans and expect that to become the standard sales plan in the future. Figure 2-5 summarizes our EVA-based incentives.

Incentive Plans	% of Incentive Compensation Tied to EVA				
	Year 1	Year 2	Year 3	Year 4	Year 5
Leadership Plan	0%	40%	80%	90%	100%
Key Assignment Plan	N/A	N/A	80%	80%	100%
Sales Commissions	0%	0%	0%	*	**
Gainsharing Plan (other associates)	0%	0%	80%	80%	100%

*One business group tied some of their sales plans to EVA.

**Two business groups tied some of their sales plans to EVA.

Figure 2-5.   EVA-based incentives

Most recently, we have adopted an Acxiom version of the Stern Stewart EVA incentive plan. This system ensures that what is good for leaders and associates reaps even bigger rewards for shareholders. At Acxiom we have validated, with Stern Stewart's assistance, that we are paying out less than 10% of the total EVA generated over time as incentives to our leaders and associates. The remainder of this return goes to earnings to build shareholder value. We also validate our EVA growth and improvement targets each fiscal year against the expected future growth in EVA by the financial community to justify our stock price. This exercise is designed to ensure that the EVA targets we set for ourselves are in sync with our stock price as well as our expectations for continued growth in returns to shareholders.

The Stern Stewart incentive system provides for unlimited upside and downside attainment of incentives. Overachievement (attainment above target) and negative attainment are booked through an incentive bank. The incentive bank is used to ensure that the incentives are matched to long-term success and not just limited to an individual year. Only a third of any positive bank balance is paid out in any one year with the remaining two-thirds being banked against future sustained performance. Any negative bank balances must be recovered in future years before incentives are paid. All of these features of the Stern Stewart incentive system combine to ensure that the incentive systems are sound for the shareholders as well as rewarding the right behavior for the associates and leaders of Acxiom.

Business Results

The ultimate goal of all internal initiatives for a company should be to improve business results. We believe that the Acxiom quality initiative and the resulting business culture, supported by ABM and with EVA tied to incentives, has met that test.

Acxiom has experienced consistent growth in EVA generated, which has also resulted in growth in traditional financial measures. We have seen a 34% compounded growth rate in revenue and a 51% compounded growth rate in earnings per share in the last five years.

Acxiom has set corporate goals in three areas: yearly growth in EVA, 100% customer satisfaction, and 100% associate satisfaction. Business results for Acxiom must be measured against these three corporate goals. We have already mentioned success with our financial goals. We have also made progress toward achieving our customer satisfaction and associate satisfaction goals.

The improvements we have made in all three corporate goals have been major factors supporting Acxiom's growth and overall return to shareholders. This is the ultimate measure of the success of the initiatives described in this case study.

Future Developments

We will continuously improve and refine all of the initiatives described in this case study. We update our EVA growth targets and incentive plans annually. Every few years, we review and update our corporate goals and initiatives to support them. And we periodically review and update our corporate structure to ensure that we are aligned to support future growth.

We have recently completed a realignment of Acxiom into four divisions. This realignment is designed to help Acxiom become a multibillion dollar company. The last major realignment occurred approximately six years ago and was intended to support Acxiom in becoming a $500 million company. Now that this goal is in sight for the coming fiscal year, it is appropriate to update our alignment. We have realigned into three U.S. divisions and one international division. The Acxiom International Division is based in London and today primarily supports the United Kingdom and Europe. We have also recently opened an office in Malaysia to begin expansion into the Asia Pacific region.

The three U.S. divisions are the Acxiom Services Division, Acxiom Alliances Division, and Acxiom Data Products Division. Each of these divisions generates more than $100 million in revenue today. We believe that all of these, as well as our international division, have the potential to grow to $500 million businesses. In many ways, we think of each of these divisions as Acxiom look-alikes five years ago.

We will continue our quality journey, develop and refine our business culture and our ABM and EVA measurement system, and apply them to each of these divisions. Each division will be offered strong incentives to contribute growth in EVA. However, we will maintain a strong common-fate component of our incentive systems to ensure that we maximize cooperative efforts between divisions and link rewards to the success of the whole Acxiom Corporation.

We believe these initiatives have laid a good foundation for Acxiom and will continue to support our successful journey.

III.

MANUFACTURING COST MANAGEMENT: A PRACTICAL LIFE-CYCLE COST PERSPECTIVE

GLENN UMINGER
Manager, Production Control
Toyota Motor Manufacturing, North America

T O UNDERSTAND MANUFACTURING cost management, you must first think in terms of total life-cycle manufacturing costs from a macro viewpoint, then understand the source and real control points of those costs. Only with this understanding are you prepared to establish the most effective methods to control total manufacturing costs. Cost control methods may vary depending on the type of product and manufacturing process required, but the principles of effective cost control remain the same. This case study provides a practical life-cycle cost perspective and a framework with key points that can help any manufacturing organization manage and control total life-cycle costs.

Traditional (i.e., Ineffective) Cost Management

My experience suggests that traditional management accounting techniques of reporting, variance analysis, and feedback are not an effective way to improve manufacturing cost performance for the following reasons:

- **Lack of timeliness.** The information arrives too late at the real activity control point. Data that is a week or a month old offers little value to the here-and-now environment of manufacturing.

- **Lack of understanding.** Having data processed by a group that resides outside the manufacturing area with limited knowledge of the floor operations creates a need for translation and interpretation that wastes time and energy.

- **No direct connection.** Traditional management accounting information says nothing about the activities or the resource consumption that actually cause costs. It only reports consequences.

- **Lack of respect for workforce.** Third party involvement, referred to above, ignores the vast contribution to cost improvement that can come from the ideas of production workers themselves.

- **Narrow perspective.** Traditional management accounting focuses only on production costs, ignoring opportunities that a total life-cycle perspective captures.

A Better Way: Focus on the Cost Control Points

Management accounting can be extremely valuable if it understands and focuses on the following cost control points, which represent windows of opportunity to directly affect costs. Management accounting needs to understand this perspective to effectively lead efforts to achieve company-wide cost objectives. Three critical cost control points collectively create the total life-cycle manufacturing costs of any product:

- Product design
- Process design
- Manufacturing operations

Only a deep understanding of each cost control point and the relationships among them will support effective cost control. Figure 3-1 lists various costs that are affected at each control point.

Note that most costs are locked in by product design and process design before the first unit is ever produced. Thus, it is critical to implement an effective process to monitor the cost impact of both product and process design. Equally important in optimizing manufacturing operation costs is an environment on the production floor that is conducive to continuous cost reduction.

Only Cost Is in Your Control

Manufacturing has to be highly competitive, considering that the market determines the price of manufactured

Cost Control Point	Cost Item	How Impacted
Product Design	Raw material	Material specification, standard quantity
	Purchased component	Part design, specifications, manufacturability
	Labor	Product complexity, manufacturability
	Building	Product complexity
	Machinery and equipment	Manufacturing requirements
	Tooling	Complexity of individual parts, number of parts
	Number of component parts	Product complexity (efficiency of design)
Process Design	Labor	Efficiency of layout (minimize nonvalue-added movements)
	Building	Efficiency of layout (compact process)
	Machinery and equipment	Specification (use existing machinery and equipment as much as possible)
	Operating efficiency	Continuous flow (to reveal problems as they occur)
Manufacturing Operations	Labor	Daily efficiencies, process improvements
	Quality costs	Daily performance
	Raw material	Quantity used
	Indirect materials	Quantity used
	Repairs and maintenance	Effective preventive maintenance program
	Operating efficiency	Systematic problem solving and improvement

Figure 3-1.   Cost impact by control point

products based on consumers' perceived value. This leaves only the cost variable of the profit equation in a manufacturing company's direct control. Thus, it is critical to maximize all cost management opportunities.

This is the same situation for each of your competitors (unless one has patented unique technology). Thus, the winners are the ones who best recognize these cost control points and skillfully administer processes that minimize total life-cycle cost.

Of course, quality is also essential for success and is a parallel part of a product's life cycle. The methods of life-cycle cost management can help companies improve quality too.

Each cost control point requires a special focus supported by a systematic process. The three cost control points should be interactive, with each providing input and receiving feedback. They represent an endless step-by-step generational flow (see Figure 3-2). Learning, development, and improvement should take place at each step in each generation. When you consider that most new products are variations or improvements to some existing product, this generational approach is easy to understand.

It is necessary to link the processes for each cost control point to provide input and receive feedback when

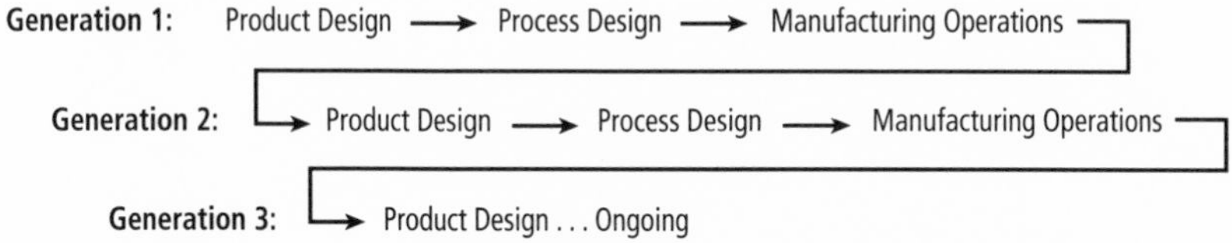

Generation 1:   Product Design ⟶ Process Design ⟶ Manufacturing Operations ⌐

Generation 2:   ⌐→ Product Design ⟶ Process Design ⟶ Manufacturing Operations ⌐

Generation 3:   ⌐→ Product Design . . . Ongoing

Figure 3-2.   Generational flow of cost control points

relevant. Manufacturability, for example, is directly affected by design, which affects cost.

Cost Control Point 1: Product Design

Most new products are variations of existing products. Even products that are considered to be completely new usually have some relation to an existing product. The key point is that product design, including cost control, can be founded on the principle of generational increments, which uses existing knowledge about the product and minimizes new variables. For example, a new model refrigerator is most likely a variation of an old one with some improvements (such as a new shelf design) or new features (such as an ice crusher in the door). As a strategy, using the current model as a basis and focusing only on the change greatly minimizes the margin of error in achieving objectives. The result is a "new" product developed with the highest chance for overall success including profitability.

To link the design process with the profit objective, it is important at the beginning of product design to connect the target for total life-cycle cost (target cost) to a target selling price to achieve the marketing plan's profit objective. Based on the change in product features and marketing research, a plus/minus price change from a similar existing product is established. Using a targeted margin ratio, a cost change allowance can be easily calculated. This can serve as the budget for the new product's target cost, as shown in Figure 3-3.

	Current Product	Change Per Marketing Plan	New Product	Cost Target
Selling Price	$1,000	+ 100	$1,100	
Cost	$ 850		$ 935	+85 +95 New Features −10 Cost Reduction
Margin	$ 150		$ 165	
Margin %	15.0%		15.0%	

Note: The cost target can be adjusted if there is a need to alter the percentage margin.

Figure 3-3.   Target cost calculation

In this example, the cost target (+ $85) would be allocated in detail over the cost elements of the current product. It is implied that additional features will exist on this new product, thus commanding a higher selling price. Therefore, most of this cost increase would be applied to the new features. If features were reduced or aggressive cost reduction was sought, a cost decrease budget would be established. In any scenario, cost reduction of the core product should be an objective and built into the allocation as an integral part of a continuous improvement culture to gain competitiveness over the long run.

Beginning with the target cost, a cost control process should parallel the design process. Periodic cost estimates and summaries should be completed to check the new product's cost position to the target cost. Feedback and necessary adjustments will ensure that the product is designed to the target cost. This very involved process is critical to life-cycle manufacturing costs. Without this process, natural cost increase pressures could take over.

Design engineers are motivated to a product's highest capability and durability. Marketing specialists are motivated to include many features. Cost problems need to be identified during the design stage, when appropriate adjustments can be made before costs are locked in.

Cost Control Point 2: Process Design

Process design impacts cost in two ways: equipment planning and process layout. From a cost perspective, effective equipment planning is easier said than done. While the design process has established what needs to be done, how the work is done is still a significant issue. The first criterion is whether the work (each specific process) should be done by a machine or a person. Having the work done by a machine just for the sake of automation is not always the better choice. You should evaluate worker-versus-machine process by process. Decision criteria include efficiency, ergonomics, and quality. When a machine is selected, the next decision is whether to use an existing machine or purchase a new one. Of course, using an existing machine is the better choice whenever possible, but it takes a company culture and a controlled process to buy flexible equipment and then maintain the equipment in "like new" condition. Without these prerequisites, the use of existing equipment may not be an option. There is also a tendency to purchase new. People making the evaluations are human and, without a sound process and culture, some may recommend new equipment justifying it as "the old equipment is fully depreciated," "we have a budget for this," or "I want this new technology."

If the proper decision is to buy new equipment, it is necessary to buy versatile equipment but no greater capability than what is needed to do the work. Again, it is human nature to want bigger and better, and the equipment salesperson usually wants to sell the same. A sound selection and approval process and a good culture is needed. Although an equipment budget must be established as part of the cost target, it is difficult to ensure that cost has been minimized without clear decision criteria and a controlled decision process.

The process layout has a significant impact on manufacturing operations cost. To minimize space, the process should be laid out very compactly. Compactness has the benefit of labor efficiency by minimizing wasted motion, with work passed directly from process to process. The most critical objective for the process layout, however, is to create a production chain that establishes a continuous flow environment in which work in progress is always due at the next process with virtually no waiting time. In such an environment, problems can be immediately detected and corrected on the production floor. This creates a very progressive environment where every break in the production chain is viewed as an opportunity to improve, rather than allowing the problem to remain as waste in the system until a report identifies a problem. In other words, the process design is the prerequisite for an environment of continuous improvement. Good process design breaks the production chain into segments connected by "rubber bands" or small controlled inventory buffers that can expand and contract to permit one segment to stop its production flow to fix a problem without directly affecting the entire production chain.

Cost Control Point 3: Manufacturing Operations

Although manufacturing operations control only a small percentage of the life-cycle cost, manufacturing is still a critical phase in life-cycle cost control for two reasons: (1) Because of low margins and the competitive environment, a great product plan and design could be offset if manufacturing operations do not meet expectations; and (2) much can be learned and improved with a progressive manufacturing environment. This results in improved manufacturing efficiency as well as improved future product and process designs.

The most important aspect of the manufacturing operations cost control point is to establish and nurture an environment that places responsibility and expectations in the hands of the people doing the work and provides feedback to them at the point of action. Problems must be viewed as opportunities, identified instantly as they occur, and solved immediately in process.

Keys to the ideal work environment include:

- **Continuous work flow.** Work is passed directly from process to process.

- **Standardization.** Each process has a work standard that serves as a foundation to identify abnormalities.

- **Visual control.** Information is readily available to production employees as they work.

- **Abnormalities are identified.** Tools are provided to determine immediately when something is out of standard (abnormal), and the culture encourages identification of the abnormality.

- **Problem-solving support.** Support is available to immediately fix the abnormality in process and to follow up with a permanent solution if the problem repeats.

- **Focus.** All activities focus on directly controllable performance measures.

- **A motivated workforce.** Production workers are motivated to control and improve their own workplace supported by management, quality circles, suggestion systems, and so on.

Establishing this environment is far from simple. It requires consistency and dedication beginning with top management and applied consistently by all management levels every minute of every day. The production workers must feel secure in their role to identify problems and ask for help without fear. They must know they will be completely supported. The workforce must also be organized to provide some floating positions so that someone is there to "run to the problem" when it occurs and help correct it.

Production workers must be sincerely respected as the experts in the company at their jobs. And they must be given all of the information, tools, and support necessary to do their jobs. Nonperforming production workers identify themselves in certain ways and can be addressed individually. Peer groups tend to be the first to identify performance issues.

It takes time, patience, consistency of action, and dedication to establish such an environment. Once established, this environment becomes the core strength of manufacturing operations and can become a significant competitive advantage.

The New Role of Management Accounting

Management accounting will always be a vital part of an organization. In this new, more productive and focused work environment, there is a significant shift in the management accountant's role from the "bad guy" or "cost enforcer" to the "knowledgeable friend" of production operations able to provide valuable support.

Key responsibilities should include:

1. **For product design and process design.** Work with the related groups to establish a process to evaluate, provide focus, and confirm cost concurrent with the design process. Administer these processes during design and provide value-added feedback and direction to ensure attainment of target costs.

2. **For manufacturing operations.** Gain an in-depth understanding of the production process. Assist in establishing additional cost control tools where necessary to ensure a manufacturing floor environment of real-time total awareness and control of all controllable costs. Provide summary and trend reports for use only as periodic confirmation of cost control achievement. Limit detailed cost analyses to focused improvement projects only. Avoid cyclical reports and analyses that do not help control cost.

3. **For senior management.** Provide periodic summary and trend reports that serve as a health report on the business from a macro viewpoint. Identify by exception the positive activities that occur within the operation and the significant improvement activities that are needed or in progress.

Summary

Focusing on these three cost control points in a practical manner is vital to success. Understanding this is only the beginning. Developing and maintaining a culture and processes to execute control methodically is the most difficult part. Depending on the starting point, it could take considerable time and effort to migrate to this environment. It requires a sound long-term plan, commitment, and patience. All cost-related activities need to be reviewed from a value-added perspective. For example, is it more important to allocate overhead accurately or to actually reduce overhead costs? Would I like a monthly financial report with 30 perfectly calculated and explained variances, or would I rather have improved cost-control tools and core production performance improvement that perpetuates itself daily? Should design and process engineering be independent activities or linked to ensure that everything is well organized and coordinated to achieve the common objective?

The benefits of refocusing increase as you proceed step by step, continuously improving over time. But if there is not a firm organizational commitment beginning at the top, efforts to change will become another failed program. This commitment to change must take precedence over an individual's preference. It cannot succeed if it is subject to significant change as individuals change positions within the organization. Once on track, the competitive advantage and rewards will be substantial.

IV.

EVA: Engine of Growth for Briggs & Stratton

President and Chief Operating Officer

AFTER SUFFERING ITS FIRST LOSS since before the Great Depression, managers at Briggs & Stratton turned to EVA to help turn the company around. The results? A newfound capital-consciousness and record profitability.

Sometimes, a little success can be a dangerous thing. We found this out the hard way at Briggs & Stratton. Ever since the company was listed on the New York Stock Exchange in 1929, Briggs & Stratton has always made a profit, even during the Depression years. We were kind of like the lightweight, gasoline-powered engines we manufactured—sturdy and reliable.

When you're recording profits year after year, you can't imagine that anything is wrong with your company, but as we painfully discovered a few years ago, something *was* wrong with our company. Although we made money, we were also spending it like mad. For one thing, our labor costs were way out of whack, nearly a third higher than that of our competitors. What's more, thanks to a costly automation program, capital tied up in operating assets had tripled over a 10-year period. Cash flow, on the other hand, barely rose. Steadily, over the years, we had accumulated a lot of cash without realizing that it had a cost. Certainly, our metric for corporate performance, earnings per share, didn't alert us to our poor capital management.

Around the same time, the competitive landscape had begun to shift. For years, Briggs & Stratton had dominated the lightweight, air-cooled engine business. Mostly, our engines went into power lawnmowers. In fact, our share of the domestic market for outdoor power equipment consistently topped 50%.

In the old days, when a consumer wanted to buy a lawnmower, he or she would go to the local John Deere store. With the mass marketization of the industry, however, Americans soon began purchasing their power mowers from discount stores such as Wal-Mart and K-Mart. For the Wal-Marts of the world, price was the prime consideration in deciding what line of lawnmowers to carry. Not surprisingly, the prices of mass-market models barely increased. The big discount retailers had even stopped giving us inflation increases. In this brave new world of discount retailers, we had little choice but to hold the line on prices. The price of our Classic engine, for instance, went up a mere 2.5% during this 10-year period. It's hard to make money off that.

In addition, we started to get competition from powerful Japanese rivals. With a weakening yen, they started flying lazy circles over the remaining consumer dealer brands. In a short while, Kawasaki made off with our John Deere contract, Suzuki took Toro, and Fuji snapped up Snapper.

All things considered, it should have come as no surprise that Briggs & Stratton finally had a losing year. In fact, we lost $20 million. For a company with revenues of more than $875 million, a $20 million loss may not sound earth-shattering. After six decades of profits, however, this loss came as a wake-up call. Suddenly, we realized that we had a serious problem on our hands that would not go away with minor fixes. We had to step back, examine what we were doing, and find a new approach to our business if we did not want to risk losing market share, and ultimately, investors. We certainly had not been rewarding our loyal shareholders during this period. While we paid a healthy dividend, our stock price had languished throughout. Our shareholders deserved a much healthier return.

Overhauling the Engine

So what did we do? We overhauled the company. For the first time in the history of Briggs & Stratton, we broke the company down into seven stand-alone divisions. We gave each unit its own general manager with reasonable autonomy. The units were also assigned their own capital to produce a defined range of engines. In addition, the manufacturing process in each division was radically altered, with cutting-edge focus factories and cell manufacturing replacing the company's historic, Tayloristic batch

51

approach. Over the years, batch processing had led to a blurred focus on cost and a huge buildup of inventory—not exactly an ideal combination. We needed to skinny down, to shed the "crank-out-the-inventory" approach that had become standard operating procedure at our giant Burleigh plant outside of Milwaukee.

However, the changes didn't stop there. We also decided we needed a new performance metric, one that would accurately monitor the management of capital in the new divisions. We didn't want to fall back into the old trap of turning a profit while frittering away capital. After all, capital isn't free. It comes from somewhere—in our case, 75% of the capital comes from institutional investors. So if you're really going to create value for your investors, you need to generate an adequate return on their investment. Remember, investors can get 7% on their money just by investing in long-term Treasury bonds—risk free.

Going EVA

After meeting with managers at Stern Stewart, a New York–based consulting firm, we decided to adopt economic value added (EVA) as our new performance metric. EVA supplants more traditional accounting measures like earnings per share and return on shareholder investment. By our lights, those measures are of less interest to providers of capital than cash-flow generation and effective capital management. While EVA has gained a reputation as a tough capital discipline—and rightly so—we liked EVA because it focuses on value creation. The central tenant of

EVA is that you're not creating value for your capital providers—a company's lenders and shareholders—unless you generate a return beyond what they could expect for similar investments (i.e., the cost of capital). Basically, EVA works like this. You determine your total capital and then the cash-adjusted operations earnings from those invest-ments. If the returns are higher than the outlays—including the weighted average cost of capital—then you have gener-ated real value for the providers of that capital. If that all sounds fairly simple, it is. Indeed, one prominent fund manager has called EVA "the codification of common sense." In the midwest, we're big on common sense.

Figure 4-1 shows our EVA calculations for the first and third year after adopting the metric. As you can see, our economic return on capital in the first year was 7.7%. That sounds good until you realize our cost of capital was 12%. Therefore, even though our balance sheet showed a net profit for the year, we lost money for our providers of capital, who could have expected a 12% return from simi-lar investments. Obviously, we needed to generate a return higher than 12% to create value for our shareholders, and we fell far short of that. By the third year, our economic return on capital was 12.9%. Our cost of capital, however, was still right around 12%. Thus, we had exceeded what our capital providers could have expected from similar investments. In short, we had created value for them.

But we went beyond just adopting EVA as our corporate yardstick. We also linked the bonus plans of senior managers to the EVA performance of Briggs &

	Year One	Year Three
Net Operating Profit After Taxes	$ 40,703,000	$ 72,431,000
Weighted Average of Capital Employed	$528,923,000	$562,209,000
Economic Return on Capital	7.7%	12.9%
Cost of Capital*	12.0%	12.0%

*Management's estimate of the weighted average of the minimum equity and debt returns required by the providers of capital

Figure 4-1.   First- and third-year EVA calculations

Stratton and the individual divisions within the company. We started by setting target incentive ranges for managers, anywhere from 20% to 80% of that executive's base pay. To hit the target, the company, along with that executive's division, must meet the EVA improvement targets set for that year (which is given a multiplier of 1). If that target is met, we multiply the bonus percentage by 1, and the executive receives the full target bonus. If the company does even better than the EVA target, the multiplier is increased—and the executive gets an even bigger bonus. Conversely, if we have a bad EVA year, the multiplier is decreased, and the executive receives a smaller bonus. EVA bonuses for the executive group are uncapped.

Part of the payoff for EVA-based bonus packages for key executives comes in the form of leveraged stock options, exercisable after a five-year period. That five-year tenure is crucial, since the managers only go "in the money" when the share price increase over that time period exceeds the cost of capital. This wrinkle keeps us squarely fixed on what's truly important—fostering long-term growth. If the share price of our stock doesn't do well over a five-year period, we'll get hit right in the wallet, just like our shareholders.

EVA As a Divining Rod

We can't think of a better way to foster sound capital management than to link executive compensation to EVA performance. For us, EVA is more than just a gauge of past performance. We use it as a divining rod for every major corporate decision we face. EVA analysis tells what product lines to get rid of and what new products to introduce. EVA guides our capital equipment purchases. It also tells us if the construction of new plants makes economic sense. This might come as a surprise, since some critics charge EVA with discouraging expenditures of any sort. To me, that's nonsense on stilts. In fact, within five years of adopting EVA, we had finished construction on four new focus factories in the United States. The total cost was $120 million. That's hardly parsimony.

On the other hand, EVA has also influenced our decisions to sell off assets. A few years after going EVA, we decided to spin off our Strattec automotive lock division. This was not an easy decision. Briggs & Stratton had been in the automotive parts business since 1909. But our numbers showed that, as a division within Briggs & Stratton, Strattec would not be able to maximize its market value added (MVA). Yet, as a stand-alone company, Strattec could generate substantial EVA growth. Ultimately, we spun the company off to our investors, further enhancing shareholder value.

EVA has also become a guiding light on our factory floors. Many of our shop workers have attended our in-house EVA seminar and are familiar with the concept of value creation. We encourage our workers to make any suggestions they think will enhance value. In our Ravenna, Michigan, foundry, for example, two maintenance workers noticed that a buildup of returns from the casting process was causing the casting machinery to jam. After studying the problem, the two employees determined that the culprit was a magnetic separator that lifted the returns from a vibratory conveyor and loaded them onto another conveyor for discharge into return bins. The two workers suggested extending the vibratory conveyor, thereby eliminating the need for the magnetic separator entirely. The scheme not only reduced the downtime caused by jams; it also enabled us to sell the separator. The sale added to our cash flow and reduced the capital employed in the factory.

Thanks to insights from employees in our Burleigh plant, we were also able to cut our inventory costs on perishable tools by 82%. How? Workers on the shop floor suggested that we agree to consign all of our business to one tool representative. In turn, the tool vendor agreed to carry the tool inventory on his balance sheet. That way, we eliminated the carrying costs for the inventory. That's a huge EVA-driver for Briggs & Stratton. So is the significant reduction we have achieved in the amount of work in progress (WIPS) on the assembly lines. Fewer WIPS means less cost and better quality control. EVA has also guided us in our decision to outsource certain tasks, which, in turn, has reduced our capital expenditures. All of this adds up to good business.

Numbers Don't Lie

It's hard to argue with the results. A year after the corporate divisionalization and the adoption of EVA, our company returned to profitability, and in the ensuing years, we saw substantial growth in our corporate earnings. One year, we topped the $100 million mark in net income, for the first time in the history of the company (see Figure 4-2). What's more, the share price of our stock has skyrocketed (see Figure 4-3). Within five years of the big changes, the Briggs & Stratton common share price more than tripled in value. That's the kind of performance that puts a hop in the step of most shareholders.

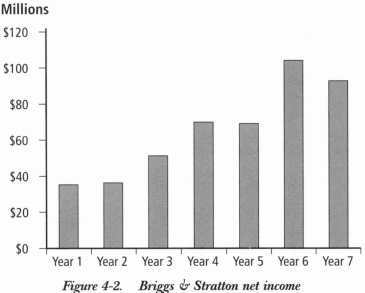

Figure 4-2. Briggs & Stratton net income since the adoption of EVA

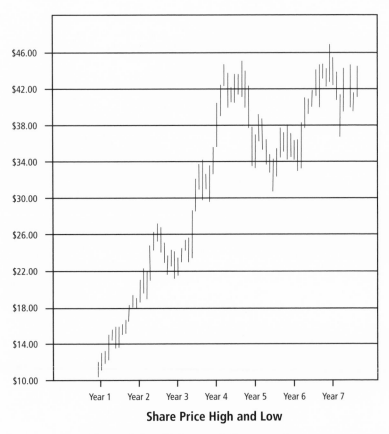

Share Price High and Low

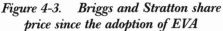

Figure 4-3. Briggs and Stratton share price since the adoption of EVA

Now, I won't say that EVA is entirely responsible for the recent success at Briggs & Stratton. The divisionalization and the switch to focus factories and cell manufacturing have also played a big part in our turnaround. In addition, the weather's been pretty good over the past few years. That's right, the weather. Warm, wet weather means lots of grass, and lots of grass means mowing. At Briggs & Stratton, we like more mowing.

Still, it's hard to get around the fact that EVA has made a huge difference in our company. Simply put, we have become much better stewards of capital, thanks to EVA. The numbers don't lie. In the year of our record profit, for example, we employed $660 million in capital. Our net adjusted cash operating profit after taxes was $116.5 million. Our cost of capital (the minimum equity and debt return required by our providers) was 11.7% for that year. A little math shows, however, that we had generated a whopping 17.6% return on capital. At that point, you're not just turning a profit. You're creating real value for shareholders. And that, to us, is what EVA is all about.

V.

Using Activity-Based Management to Foster Growth: The Alpha Industries Experience

Paul Therrien
Operations Controller, Alpha Industries, Inc.

Bruce Baggaley
President, Baggaley Consulting, Inc.

MANY MANAGERS THINK that achieving company growth is independent of control of operations. However, in the warp-speed environment of the infocom industry in which sales growth of 20% to 30% is the norm, effective control of operating processes means that everyone in the organization must operate at warp speed. The Alpha Industries, Inc. case shows how one company is transforming to meet these heightened demands for growth. It demonstrates the absolute necessity of clearly articulated business strategies and goals for focused, effective performance measurement.

The Business Challenge

Alpha Industries is a $100 million-per-year manufacturer of semiconductors to the wireless, nonwireless, and military communications markets. While its traditional market is military, it aspires to be a leading supplier of semiconductors to the wireless market, which is projected to grow at 27% per year through the year 2000. To meet this goal, Alpha developed state-of-the-art chip technology. The company has transformed its manufacturing process to meet the demands for producing chips at the required rates. In spite of these initiatives, it had not been able to increase its rate of growth in sales to meet the opportunities presented by the expanding market. Alpha's growth in wireless sales for fiscal year 1996 was only 6%, notwithstanding high growth in the two previous years.

Anticipating the need for change, management decided in 1995 that it needed to take a business process approach to managing all of its business processes, not just manufacturing. Using *activity-based management* (ABM) methods, the company would begin with a pilot study of all the activities required to fulfill an order—taking the order; planning the fulfillment; making silicon wafers; assembling and testing the diodes; and shipping, billing, and collecting the cash. Management selected cycle time, throughput, cost, and quality as the criteria against which to monitor performance of the entire business process.

Content and Organization
of the ABM Pilot

Activity-based management is financial management based on units of work called activities. This approach is radically different from the traditional accounting framework, which is based on resources used, such as labor, material, and overhead. The rationale is to manage costs by managing the drivers, or causes, of the work performed, rather than the capacity to perform the work (for example, by reducing the number of employees).

The pilot had three objectives:

- To demonstrate the applicability of the ABM principles to Alpha Industries

- To identify, using ABM techniques, the potential for cost savings and process improvement to eliminate obstacles to meeting wireless customer demands

- To establish activity-based performance measures to monitor improvement progress

The ABM pilot was performed over a three-month period and included five major tasks:

- Project planning—refining pilot objectives, assembling the team, and establishing the detailed work plan.

- Activity analysis—identifying and describing activities through departmental workshops.

- Activity accounting—relating resources (computers, equipment, utilities, space, and the like) to activities by estimating the percentage of total available departmental resource capacity that was employed by the activities in a department during the period of study.

- Continuous improvement monitoring–using the activity cost data developed in the previous tasks and identifying the costs of activities that were obstacles to customer satisfaction, the root causes of these activities, and the potential initiatives to eliminate the causal factors. And finally, developing a performance measurement framework to monitor improvement progress.

- Plan for full implementation of ABM beyond the pilot–establishing the time frame for rolling out ABM to other business processes, such as new product development.

Figure 5-1 outlines the ABM methodology which was based on techniques developed by Integrated Cost Management Systems of Arlington, Texas.

The pilot organization consisted of a leader who spent 75% of his time on the project for the duration of the pilot. Team members from each of the major departments responsible for order fulfillment–including sales, marketing, engineering, wafer fabrication manufacturing, assembly manufacturing, manufacturing planning, and accounting–spent from 25% to 50% of their time on the project. Others, such as quality and statistical process control, data processing, and department personnel, spent 5% to 10% of their time on the project. All sessions were conducted in line with the company's policy of involving as many people as possible in making change happen.

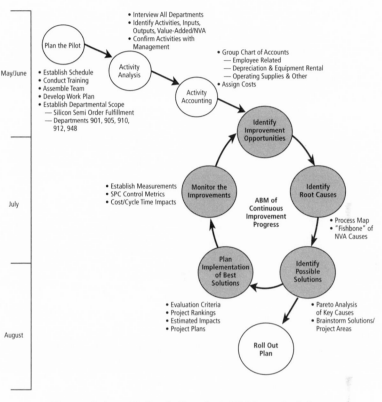

Figure 5-1.   Alpha Industries' ABM methodology

Key Pilot Findings

The pilot team found that much of the work performed
in order fulfillment did not contribute to meeting customer
requirements but was undertaken to overcome or correct
failures in processing customers' orders. In fact, of the
40 activities identified in order fulfillment, 22 were judged
to create no value for customers (see boxed areas in
Figure 5-2).

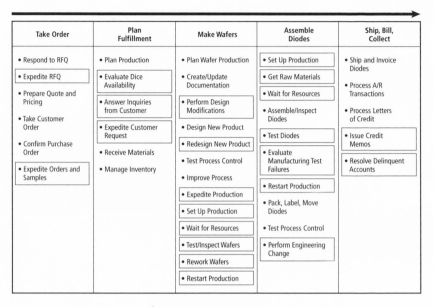

Take Order	Plan Fulfillment	Make Wafers	Assemble Diodes	Ship, Bill, Collect
• Respond to RFQ	• Plan Production	• Plan Wafer Production	• Set Up Production	• Ship and Invoice Diodes
• Expedite RFQ	• Evaluate Dice Availability	• Create/Update Documentation	• Get Raw Materials	• Process A/R Transactions
• Prepare Quote and Pricing	• Answer Inquiries from Customer	• Perform Design Modifications	• Wait for Resources	• Process Letters of Credit
• Take Customer Order	• Expedite Customer Request	• Design New Product	• Assemble/Inspect Diodes	• Issue Credit Memos
• Confirm Purchase Order	• Receive Materials	• Redesign New Product	• Test Diodes	• Resolve Delinquent Accounts
• Expedite Orders and Samples	• Manage Inventory	• Test Process Control	• Evaluate Manufacturing Test Failures	
		• Improve Process	• Restart Production	
		• Expedite Production	• Pack, Label, Move Diodes	
		• Set Up Production	• Test Process Control	
		• Wait for Resources	• Perform Engineering Change	
		• Test/Inspect Wafers		
		• Rework Wafers		
		• Restart Production		

Figure 5-2.   Twenty-two activities in order fulfillment were judged to be nonvalue added

As Figure 5-2 suggests, a chain of causation created obstacles to efficient order fulfillment:

- The sales department booked large numbers of orders for small runs of specialized semiconductors without sufficient understanding either of the specific requirements or of Alpha's ability to deliver on those requirements before taking the orders

- Excessive research regarding the availability of existing "dice," used to make the chips, after taking the order

- Multiple design modifications and redesign of wafers to meet customers' specialized needs

- Excessive time to learn how to make these new designs, requiring specialized skills of engineers that are in short supply

- Excessive time in assembly to make semiconductors that conform to customer requirements

- Excessive time to respond to questions from angry customers related to late delivery and to expedite production of their orders

- Excessive time to collect the amounts due from customers that had received their shipments late or not exactly in accordance with their specifications

The pilot also showed that this chain of causation added $624 or 42% to the cost of the average order. The greatest costs were due to not having the right kinds of resources available to make the orders and quality control associated with nonconformance to customer requirements.

The low average order size suggested that Alpha was accepting too many small specialty orders, using valuable capacity that might have been employed by orders from larger customers that were more in line with Alpha's strategy to be a leading producer for the wireless market.

Not only did the pilot reveal the problems with order profitability and size, but it also revealed a relatively poor cycle time performance, regardless of the importance of the business to Alpha. Order-to-shipment cycle time averaged 32 days. Even routine catalog orders took 28 days.

These findings suggested a lack of communication and integration of the company's business strategy into product-market and operating strategies and policies throughout the order-fulfillment process, from preorder to delivery. They also suggested that the lack of integration and focus was creating obstacles to achieving the company's business strategy and growth objectives.

To confirm these findings, Alpha conducted a survey of the largest wireless product manufacturers to assess its attractiveness to its target market as a major supplier of semiconductors. The findings suggested that the company was viewed as a "specialty" house for small supplies and not sufficiently reliable in delivering on time to be a major supplier. With the ABM results confirmed, management decided to act.

Initiating Change Programs

The ABM results combined with the survey results convinced management to make the following major changes in strategy and organization:

- Defined three market segments for focus, each requiring different product, market, and operations strategies: (1) key customers (consisting of the largest manufacturers of wireless products), (2) major accounts (consisting of high-volume customers), and (3) distributors (to handle smaller accounts). This was a major shift from the traditional practice of treating all customer groups the same.

- Reorganized around these three market segments and defined executives responsible for all aspects of order generation and fulfillment to these segments. This represented a major shift in focus from the former product focus of the organization.

- Implemented a process for coordinating sales and operations capacity planning to cope with the problems in understanding and communicating customer requirements.

- Reorganized sales channels to focus on market segments.

- Pruned unprofitable products and customers.

- Changed the measurement and reward systems to focus on customer satisfaction, not solely on internal operating performance and order volumes.

- Implemented improved systems, eliminating "islands of data" by department, so that operations can be linked to strategy throughout the order fulfillment process.

It has been approximately two years since Alpha performed the ABM pilot. It has taken that long to restructure the company so that the results of operations can be measured in a way that can be linked with strategy. Having put the structure in place, Alpha can now measure how well the company is performing by major market segment, related to cost, cycle time, quality, throughput, and return on assets employed (see Figure 5-3).

This also permits management to look at subprocesses and activities, making it possible for them to put initiatives in place to eliminate obstacles to achieving the goal of customer satisfaction.

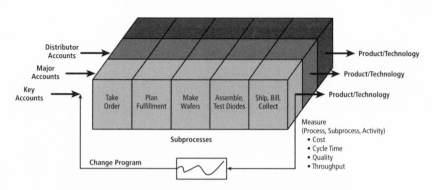

Figure 5-3.   Reorganizing by market segment enables
Alpha Industries to implement ABM aligned with strategy

Continuing Programs

Implementing the activity-based performance measurement structure is a continuing program for Alpha. It provides the basis for linking operations, financial, and strategic goals, and managing a continuous improvement process that can be implemented in real time by operations people. The results are yet to be proven, but Alpha is confident that it is positioned to manage its operations to meet the demands of rapid growth.

VI.

EXECUTIVE INFORMATION SYSTEMS AT PITNEY BOWES MAILING SYSTEMS

MARK D. GREEN
Director, Strategic Marketing Finance

MANY KNOW PITNEY BOWES as a postage machine company, but the company also sells and distributes facsimile machines, copiers, mailroom products, and shipping systems.

This chapter describes the evolution of the executive information systems in the Mailing Systems Division. Our value chain of transactions ranges from less than $15 per month to multimillion dollar contracts. We have more than 1.3 million active customers, who we invoice at various time intervals (monthly, quarterly, or annually).

From the beginning, we viewed most business information through our accounting systems. Designed in the 1970s, our systems were designed to handle a million or more transactions each day. Over time, more than 45 integrated systems were built for our accounting system to close our books each month. But, while we changed, developed, and introduced new system-related products, our management information systems related to decision support had not changed.

This report will describe our journey to developing and implementing an executive information system (EIS), selecting performance measures relative to their financial impact, and keeping track of our strategic initiatives in a balanced scorecard.

Developing the Executive Information System

Providing a multidimensional (geographic, product line, and functional) analysis has become increasingly important. While our big box information systems remained transaction oriented, we took advantage of the evolving PC revolution to become more process and analytically oriented. Management was looking for information providers, not report generators.

For instance, our analysis now focuses on the profitability of customers by market segment over time, not just by product lines at the end of the month. As senior managers become more computer literate, their requests are even greater and the information is expected to be "on the system," not on paper!

Today we have segregated the information so all key stakeholders have access to it in an easy-to-use format, from high-level summary to drill-down, which contains detailed information in user-defined queries (normally run on the mainframe), and incorporates fact-based financial and nonfinancial measures.

Finance and the information technology division organized a project to develop the needed executive information system. For several months a small task team outlined the project milestones and deliverables to complete the project by the requested due date.

To provide the information, we had to learn new skills and change analysis techniques. The skill mix for us and our employees has changed over the past few years, and we needed to be experts in several fields. We now must be able to assess the strategic outlook of the business as well as to keep the president's PC working. Our skill mix has evolved from accounting, analysis and presentation to systems, analysis, solutions and presentation.

Phase I of the project was divided into seven steps:

1. Understand customer needs

2. Measure current performance

3. Establish improvement goals

4. Apply quality tools

5. Evaluate results

6. Recognize success

7. Continuously improve

First, we had to understand the current situation. We interviewed our key managers, listened to their concerns, reviewed their wish lists, and identified the two or three key items they would like to see in the new system. We also had to go through a lot of files to learn about previous attempts at system development to understand why they failed or lost momentum. Lastly, it was imperative to ensure that we understood the correlation to our budget, objectives, and strategic plan.

We prepared a Gantt chart to identify the key items and their appropriate timing to outline our plan, identify resources, and gain management's endorsement.

Unfortunately, our twelve-month plan was shortened to five months! In order to save time, we needed to identify which of the items we could do concurrently and which of the items were dependent on another activity. To gauge whether we were successful, we developed baseline measures of current performance, either in terms of the measures in place or in terms of the drivers that influence the measures.

At first, it was hard to realize that our financials were not the leading measures of our business but rather the lagging results of how our business performed. Critical success factors such as new product development, customer survey analysis, and economic factors were items that had dramatic effects on our business.

To quantify and report on the measures, it was important to establish improvement goals based on budgets or market objectives. Improvement goals had to be identified to insure linkage to organizational strategy and to identify where cross-functional support was needed.

The system had to communicate to the organization how we are performing against our long-term objectives and our "stretch" goals. We decided on a graphical user interface (GUI) system with signals, or "traffic lights," to alert management if our objectives will be missed, deserve some attention, or are on track. Identifying the measures to incorporate into the system required some planning and the application of a quality improvement process.

Selecting and organizing the pilot team was critical. As leader, I had to keep the team going and incorporate management's desires. We learned that the importance of the project must be cascaded down from the top and reinforced by an executive champion. We had to identify everyone's role and responsibilities within the team, including the administrators, technicians, information providers, and users. The ways to measure or prioritize actions involved applying quality improvement tools and techniques, including brainstorming exercises, fishbone diagrams, and force field analyses. We also used the Pareto technique to focus our efforts on the measures that had an immediate impact and could be developed quickly.

Implementation proceeded in three phases—template, pilot, and production. This kept us on track and more importantly, helped us meet management expectations.

During implementation we needed to evaluate the results. We needed honest and important feedback, from the team, potential users, and management. Communication was important to reduce resistance to change, manage expectations, and gain management approval.

With success, we remembered to reward those who helped us get there. A key issue was how to reward individuals in a team environment. We distributed bonuses such as plaques, dinners, and references in publications—not very costly, but very effective. We are still trying to deal with the reward problem. We estimate that for every person on the team, there are seven others in the background or on their staff who assisted.

As business, environment, and focus change objectives, our system must change and adapt. In our continuous efforts to improve the system, we continually solicit feedback and work on getting good information out faster. We categorize our measures into control, operational, and strategic information. Ideally, the system will be a blend of all three, with more drill-downs for control-type information. Control measures monitor routine, ongoing processes. Operational measures provide information for operating management decision support. Strategic measures focus on the vision or long-term goals of the enterprise.

Selecting Appropriate Measures

A key part of the process involving measuring performance and establishing improvement goals is gathering the data. We gathered as much information as we could to satisfy the individual and organizational desires. We then sorted the information into the specific measures that would be part of our system. We accomplished this at a one-day off-site meeting with the people who know the data and how to get the key information: vice presidents, directors, managers, and analysts. Figure 6-1 shows the criteria we used to select our measures.

We accumulated a list of more than 500 measures from existing reports, files, and conversations. Our group

Priority Worksheet		
Criteria	1–5 Rating Scale	Project 1
Importance	1 = Extremely	3
Availability	1 = Full	2
Ease of Retrieval	1 = Easy	3
Accuracy	1 = Totally Accurate	2
Accountability	1 = One Person	2
Other	1 = Phase One	2
Totals		14

Figure 6-1.   The priority worksheet

ranked these items using the criteria shown in Figure 6-1. The measures that we agreed to use were those that got the most important (lowest) score. This is ultimately how we decided on the implementation of Phase I. It also gave us an indication of the measures for the implementation of Phases II and III.

From these measures, we implemented our pilot, on schedule. Figure 6-2 shows the screen that we believed an executive would want to see first thing in the morning. It includes large icons and a simple interface design. It is important to keep things simple and consistent. The News icon is a summary of stock price information, news articles related to Pitney Bowes, and information about the measures in the system. The Written Business icon is a report

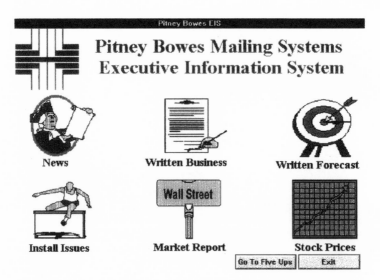

Figure 6-2. Mailing Systems Executive Information System

on our daily quota activity. The Market Report and Stock Prices icons are daily uploads of information from Wall Street analysts. Once our executives have seen the summary information, they can go into the next screen, shown in Figure 6-3, for more detail, which includes the measures in our balanced scorecard.

This screen shows the "Five Ups," the key items in our objectives. If you take care of the customers, employees, key partners, and competitors, the financials will take care of themselves. The Customer Loyalty section includes reports on how our customers feel about Pitney Bowes. It contains graphs that indicate our performance each quarter by market segment. This quick, clean presentation yields very detailed customer information from

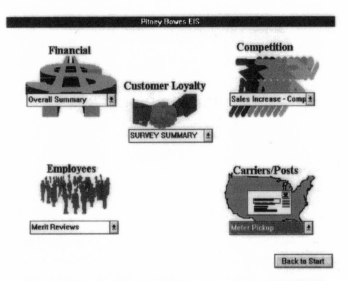

Figure 6-3.   Selecting appropriate measures "5 UPS"

40,000 surveys, focusing on the survey questions showing the largest degree of customer satisfaction. Specifically, a summary chart highlights the questions relative to importance correlated to customer satisfaction. Once the key areas are highlighted, an SAS program identifies the possible improvement in overall satisfaction that could be expected if we were to move those responses from dissatisfied to very satisfied. This provided a useful tool with which to focus improvement initiatives.

We constantly reviewed our system to ensure that we had the best measures to track our performance. Most of the measures were from the pilot list of 55 measures, which came from our original 500 measures. We tried to ensure a blend of all the five ups, working out the issues of how and where to get this information.

We considered four issues in evaluating measures— whether the data would be collected mechanically or manually, and whether the measures would be nice to have or critical to have. Critical/mechanical was our objective.

To determine which measures to implement, we made sure that a substantial number of measures came from existing systems. We didn't want to key items into Lotus or Excel spreadsheets manually. Figure 6-4 shows the main menu for our business information system listing the reports on our system that managers can review in detail.

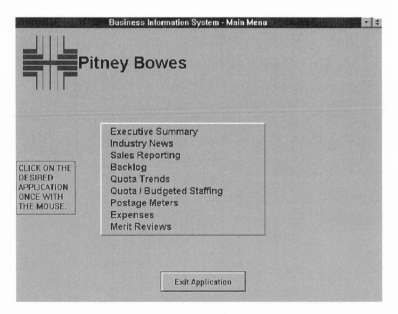

Figure 6-4. Business information system main menu

Our initial pilot used about 800 megabytes of storage; the current system uses about 8 gigabytes and growing. One of the major measures used on a daily basis is the sales reporting application. The application reviews daily a forecast for month-end revenue. Previously, we had no estimate of our sales results until after we had closed the books.

The backlog application reviews backlogs and the reasons for them by division, product line, length, units, or dollars. The backlog application is reviewed in great detail, especially toward the end of the month.

Another example of our measures is cost center expenses. These are summarized from more than 200 subaccounts and can be viewed by every functional area, department, or manager. For further analyses, these reports can be downloaded to an Excel file or printed out on a printer at work, home, or hotel room.

Over time, our EIS has become more focused (from 55 to 9 measures), has more operational measures, and now concentrates on key aspects of our business, such as quota reporting, postage meters, and overhead costs. It is flexible enough to accommodate changes if we realign businesses, products, or business units, since it is based on relational databases. We have measures that our users can view with the point-and-click of a mouse. They can even develop their own SQL queries and reports with some of the existing menus.

Summary

In summary, we have learned three things from our EIS. First, nonfinancial and financial performance measures are linked. We know that timely merit reviews are a positive influence on employee behavior. Happy and positive employees are positive and friendly to our customers, who in turn feel better about Pitney Bowes. Customer satisfaction surveys showed satisfaction was influenced by getting correct invoices and by fast response to billing inquiries. This in turn speeded up payments, reduced days outstanding by three days, and significantly improved cash flow.

Second, we constantly need to improve and renovate our performance measures and systems. By getting involved with operations, we can compare, discuss, and benchmark measures and processes to continuously improve.

The final lesson we learned has to do with system implementation. Important requirements:

- Be able to describe the technical part of the business and system in simple terms to report on it

- Use the power and low cost of PC workstations and servers versus mainframes

- Separate an EIS implementation from current accounting

- Form a project team with multiple skill sets

- Appoint a small group of full-time individuals for the initial implementation

- Recognize that a quick start-up is not a part-time job

- Eliminate; very likely one out of every two or three new measures

- Use a process improvement approach

- Make sure you can analyze early trends and have the ability to understand the business before closing the books

- Have sufficient detail built into the system

- Make sure the measures are tied to objectives

- Start by implementing a pilot and go on from there

At Pitney Bowes, we are embarking on the journey to explore our competitiveness, quantify the gap between Pitney Bowes and Best in Class, identify the major initiatives to improve our competitiveness, and set up teams to implement the necessary changes. The key details of all these initiatives include:

- Identifying gaps in meeting organizational and strategic goals through competitive analysis

- Clarifying corporate vision and gaining consensus on the key strategic initiatives

- Prioritizing, combining, and tracking initiatives to minimize gaps

- Involving the appropriate people in tracking initiatives

- Determining the appropriate measures and integrating them into the balanced scorecard

- Implementing continuous improvement efforts by performing periodic and systematic strategic reviews

- Obtaining feedback to improve upon the information systems

Figure 6-5 illustrates the continuing development of the Pitney Bowes balanced scorecard, with the intention of drastically changing the decision support mechanisms, managing change, and communicating results.

Determining the Appropriate Measures and Integrating Them into the Balanced Scorecard

Strategic Intent	Operational Strategy Development	Prioritization and Deployment	Human Resource Deployment	Performance Management
Market Share Shareholder Value Customer Satisfaction	Quality Service Cycle Time Cost Base First Run Yield	Organizational Capacity Utilization Efficiency (% Nonvalue-Added (NVA))	Percent Working on Core Processes	Strategic Goal Objectives

Figure 6-5.   The continuing development of the Pitney Bowes balanced scorecard

84

VII.

THE EVOLUTION
OF ADI'S SCORECARD

ROBERT STASEY
Director of Quality Improvement

I n 1986, ANALOG DEVICES, INC. (ADI) set in motion a
series of on-time delivery improvement strategies that
culminated in the creation of one of the industry's
most useful in-house quality improvement tools, the business scorecard. The iimprotance of the ADI scorecard will
be examined from several perspectives. First, as the creator
of the initial business scorecard, I will share the perspective
of a pioneer. Next, I will examine the linkage between the
scorecard, total quality management, and organizational
learning. Finally, I will explore ideas about the continuing
evolution of the scorecard.

Analog Devices, Inc. (ADI) was founded in 1965
in Norwood, Massachusetts, to design, manufacture, and
market monolithic integrated circuits and hybrid compo-
nents based on linear, digital, and mixed signal technology.
For 15 years ADI grew at a rate of 25% a year, becoming
a leader in data acquisition and signal processing applica-
tions in instrumentation, industrial, military, and aerospace
markets. Increasingly, ADI has focused on serving the

rapid growth markets in computers, communications, consumer, and automotive products.

Starting in 1982, company sales and profits slowed and, for the first time, ADI missed its five-year objectives. Despite technology leadership and high-quality products, the company was not meeting customer delivery commitments. Clearly, quality gains had not extended to improving on-time delivery. Additional areas of concern at the time were reducing lead times and accelerating new product introduction in targeted markets.

In 1986, Art Schneiderman, VP of Planning and Quality, gathered input from 20 associates who regularly had customer contact. Each reported that the most frequent phone call received from customers started with the question, "Where is my order?"

Establishing Measures

ADI was determined to improve on-time delivery and allocated considerable resources to generate improvement. A goal was set: "To deliver all orders complete and when promised while minimizing lateness where we fail." ADI recognized that the development and use of metrics would be necessary to monitor order fulfillment. Measures were established and a data collection system was created for causal analysis and to initiate timely corrective action.

ADI management had taken the first step toward creating the first business scorecard. Management's initial premise was to use total quality management (TQM) concepts to develop a five-year plan. ADI believed that TQM would improve the quality of both the plan and its execution; the notion of integrating business planning and TQM was set in motion. A formal business scorecard would be drafted and used to communicate key long-term goals, to cascade market strategy to all business units, and to finalize the bottom-up plans. The following list details ADI's 1987 quality improvement plan (QIP) goals:

Business Objectives:	Market leadership
	Revenue growth
	Profitability
Drivers:	Rated #1 by our customers
External Levers:	Products
	Defect levels
	On-time delivery
	Lead-time
Internal Levers:	Time to market
	Process PPM
	Manufacturing cycle time
	Yield

Measures were developed for each critical success factor. ADI identified critical success factors that were important to several key constituencies. These constituencies included stockholders, customers, employees, and process owners. (The key constituency concept later became the four sections of a balanced scorecard, popularized by Norton and Kaplan in their 1989 *Harvard Business Review* article on the ADI scorecard.)

The scorecard continued to take shape as the five-year QIP goals were created. The goals were developed by using a half-life model developed by Art Schneiderman, who observed that lasting quality improvement activity

Project Type	Examples	Model Half-Life	Expected Range
Uni-functional	Operator errors WIP	3 months	1 to 6
Cross-functional	New product cycle time	9 months	6 to 12
Multi-entity	Vendor quality, Warranty costs	16 months	12 to 24

Figure 7-1.   Half-life values

generated a constant rate of improvement over a specified time period. For example, quality defects were reduced by 50% in three months; in like manner, delays and waste in other areas had their own rate of improvement over time. Figure 7-1 lists the half-life values for some ADI improvement projects. From experience, we developed a model for determining target half-life for ADI projects (see Figure 7-2). (Schneiderman later validated his half-life concept at other companies.)

Thus, ADI goals could be determined by using the observed half-life improvement over the five years. If the extrapolated goal fell short of expectations, ADI had the choice of lowering the goal, increasing resources (teams), stretching out the deadline, or accelerating the rate of learning.

Rolling Out the First Scorecard

In 1987, the first scorecard emerged when disagreement occurred regarding a general manager meeting agenda.

Target Half-Lives, Months

Organizational Complexity			
High	14	18	22
Medium	7	9	11
Low	1	3	5
	Low	Medium	High

Technical Complexity

Figure 7-2. ADI half-life model

The COO said, "Art, the reason we are having difficulty in setting the quarterly General Manager Council agenda is that we are arguing about which comes first, financial or nonfinancial goals. Your job is to figure out how to integrate them." The business scorecard provided a means of displaying the interconnected relationship of financial and nonfinancial goals.

The scorecard became part of the five-year improvement plan beginning in 1988. Deployed to all divisions, the scorecard provided management with the performance measures—plan and actual—that would deliver satisfaction to customers, shareholders, employees, and process owners. Moreover, the relevant measures could be cascaded throughout the organization for deployment to all work groups involved. Figure 7-3 shows the first 1988 scorecard.

Three types of scorecard objectives were monitored: financial, nonfinancial, and QIP. The scorecard served as the monitoring tool to measure strategy execution quarterly. Financial measures, lagging indicators, were

Financial	FY 87 Actual	Q1 88 Plan Actual	Q2 88 Plan Actual	Q3 88 Plan Actual	Q4 88 Plan Actual	FY 88 Plan Actual
Revenue						
Revenue Growth						
Profit						
ROA						

New Products
Introductions
Bookings
Breakeven
Peak Revenue
Time to Market

QIP
On Time Delivery
Cycle Time
Yield
Defects, PPM
Cost
Employee Productivity
Turnover

Figure 7-3.   ADI's first business scorecard

place markers. Since the business strategy was to accelerate new product development, new product metrics were emphasized. QIP and nonfinancial measures served as leading indicators for planned process improvements.

What happened? In terms of order fulfillment:

- One of ADI's largest customers upgraded its assessment of ADI from "Difficult to do business with" to "Number One."

- ADI was selected as Dataquest's Mid-sized Semiconductor Supplier of the Year for the maximum two consecutive years allowable.

- Late line items improved from 30% to 4%.

In terms of quality:

- For one factory, wafer probe yield rose from 53% in 1988 to 88% in 1996.

- Outgoing quality levels, as measured by parts per million (PPM), were reduced from 2,510 to 25 PPM.

Initially, the scorecard was used to guide the company toward continuously improved performance dictated by the strategic plan. An important part of the evolution of this improvement tool was the deployment of the scorecard measures to the divisions and the further deployment of the appropriate measures to individual units and processes. In this way, the related scorecards throughout the company aligned operations with company strategy and integrated all company decisions and actions to the achievement of company goals.

Since its initiation in 1986, the ADI scorecard has gained recognition from both academics and consultants. In 1989, a Harvard Business School case was published documenting the usefulness of the ADI scorecard. In 1991, Nolan Norton established a multiclient study to seek out best practices. ADI was cited for a best practice award for its scorecard. Both of these studies summarized the scorecard's purpose and function as shown in Figure 7-4.

Concurrent with its development of the business scorecard, ADI changed its corporate culture. ADI adopted a TQM concept called *market-in,* which focuses on customer satisfaction. This is in sharp contrast to the traditional concept of *product-out,* which focuses on the

Scorecard Purpose	Why Necessary
Links business strategy to stakeholders	Financial metrics are lagging indicators
Identifies leading indicators	Focuses improvement activity
Focuses management on what's important	Links long-term and annual plans

Figure 7-4.   Purpose and function of the ADI scorecard

product rather than the customer. Companies with a product-out orientation may reject a customer's complaints by saying, "You are using our product incorrectly." In contrast, the market-in concept focuses on customer input and says the job is done well only when the customer is satisfied. All actions focus on satisfying customer expectations.

Implementing TQM

Scorecard measures as a means of communicating and monitoring the strategy are only part of the story. Tools and methods to both develop and execute a company's plan are needed. For ADI, the tools and methods are derived from our TQM philosophy. ADI has found that TQM improved both the quality of its plans and plan execution. Our experience with TQM indicated that TQM was inextricably linked to the scorecard. Without TQM, organizations would find implementing a scorecard difficult at best. (Replication of the scorecard by other companies without TQM later proved the validity of this premise.) Figure 7-5 summarizes the benefits of the linkage of TQM to the scorecard.

Figure 7-6 summarizes the ADI scorecard/TQM journey from 1983 to the present.

Our learning curve improved with the ADI scorecard/TQM journey. We learned about market-in and the many other disciplines of TQM. We learned to assume that there is always a better way. We learned how to use the right tool effectively and to find better ways of running our business. We became a learning organization. As noted by then-CEO Ray Stata: "The rate at which organizations and individuals learn may be the greatest source of competitive advantage."

Making Continuous Improvements

Once developed, a scorecard is not something that can remain static. Changing markets, more aggressive competition, and improved company performance all cause the scorecard to evolve. Moreover, improving company performance requires metric refinement. As Marshall Meyer, professor at the University of Pennsylvania, has concluded in his metric studies: "In time, all measures run down.

Importance	Performance
Improves goal setting	Improves execution
Provides the methods for achieving goals	Standardization reduces variation
Focuses improvement on the "vital few"	Improves resource allocation
Aligns the organization	Minimizes organizational conflict
Plans support the goal	Monitoring performance becomes easier

Figure 7-5.   Benefits of TQM linkage to the scorecard

	1983–1986 Self-Learning Mode	1986–1989 Staff Specialist as Facilitator	1989–1994 CEO as Leader	1995–Present Senior Managers as Champions
Motivation	"We know we can do better"	Concern with slowing growth	Fear, possible humiliation	A source of competitive advantage
Influence	Zero	Schneiderman	Shoji Shiba	Many
Orientation	Financial	Process versus results	Mutual learning	Flows from strategy
Driven by	Novices trying the do-it-yourself approach	Staff expert	Top management	Senior managers
Results	Zero	Clear progress but not smooth	Organization embraces improvement	Hunt for big game

Figure 7-6.   ADI's scorecard/TQM journey

New measures of performance must be constantly under review. Accelerated learning rates suggest we will cycle through measures with great rapidity."

Over the years, our learning has continuously changed and improved our scorecard. While ADI's scorecard has shown remarkable consistency, subtle changes in measures have evolved over time.

In our scorecard/TQM journey we have learned that, while financial measures are important indicators of success, they do not help us achieve success. Success results from other actions. The scorecard helps us to define those important other actions, the true drivers of company success. Using critical success factor measures, realistic goals can be set. TQM provides the methods for achieving these goals.

For ADI the results of employing scorecards and TQM approaches have been impressive. Figure 7-7 shows sales and operating profit performance from 1991 to 1996.

We are now working toward further improvement in all of our scorecard measures. Examples include a maniacal focus on reducing new product time to market, reducing manufacturing cycle time, and measuring customer service responsiveness. Each measure refinement or breakthrough target value reinforces our constancy of purpose and customer focus and satisfaction. We continue to learn new lessons and to communicate them effectively across the organization. We are confident that our employees' TQM skills will continue to support planned profitable growth.

To determine your company's effectiveness in communicating, executing, and monitoring your business strategy, your company may find ADI's audit questions helpful. Rank the following in terms of effectiveness, on a 1-to-5 scale (5 = Best):

- How effective is the business strategy linkage to the stakeholders?

- How effective are the business strategy leading indicators?

- How effective are the business strategy plans as measured by the goal achievement?

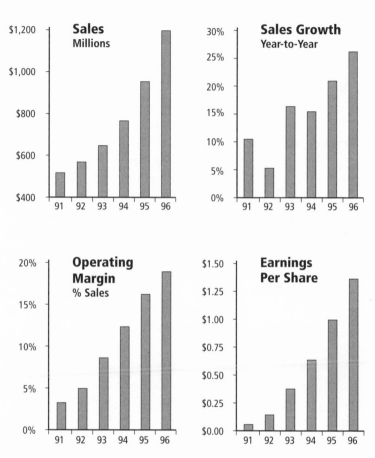

Figure 7-7. ADI's sales and operating profit performance from 1991 to 1996

- How effective are the metrics in motivating the desired management behavior?

- How effective are the metrics in measuring organizational learning?

If your company determines that opportunities for improvement exist, begin to draft your company-specific scorecard and embark on your own TQM journey.

VIII.

SUMMARY

THE REPORTS IN THIS BOOK describe an ongoing revolution in management accounting for action planning, performance measurement, and decision support. The management accounting that created past successes no longer meets the needs of today. Leading companies are developing and using better measures and methods that help people throughout the enterprise work together, combining their diverse skills to create organization success.

Some important themes:

1. The starting point is company vision made specific for everyone in the organization by strategy, values, and strategic goals that set the overall direction for company operations.

2. Measures apply to all of the organization's key performance areas–those key areas that determine organization success.

3. The most effective company culture focuses on customer value–*market-in* rather than *product-out*.

4. Measures are not only for evaluation of performance. More importantly, measures are

designed to inform all involved, as work progresses, with the information needed to achieve desired performance results. The measures are more for those doing the work than for higher level "evaluation."

5.   One result from the new management accounting will be process definition, analysis, redesign, measurement, and management, continuously improving the way work is done.

6.   The appropriate measures are needed at each level, from first level work group to the executive suite, to inform and empower those at each level with the information they need to accomplish their intended goals.

7.   The revolution in management accounting is a journey, not a destination. The journey embraces three streams of wisdom—finance and accounting, total quality management, and managerial economics.

8.   Learning, education, and training are an important part of developing best practices in each organization. Benchmarking is a useful method.

9.   The measures of the new management accounting will be used more and more in the design of incentive compensation plans.

World-class companies are leading the revolution in management accounting concepts, methods, and measures.

We can learn much from the companies reporting in this book, and from other pioneering companies and individuals. We can open our eyes to new ideas in the metrics for decision support, and for designing information systems that can help people at all levels accomplish desired results.

We will learn from finance and accounting. But we will also learn from total quality management and managerial economics. The leaders will draw from the old. But even more, they will develop and embrace the new. The revolution continues to invent a new management accounting that is essential for continuous improvement and world-class performance.

ABOUT THE AUTHORS

BRUCE BAGGALEY is president of Baggaley Consulting, Inc., in Darien, Connecticut. He specializes in the development of advanced management control processes that incorporate the principles of activity-based costing, structured systems analysis, and strategic cost management. He received his bachelors degree in economics from Dartmouth College and holds an MBA in finance from Columbia University.

MARK D. GREEN is director of strategic marketing finance at Pitney Bowes in Stamford, Connecticut. He is responsible for identifying and analyzing emerging business trends through information technology, quantitative research methods, benchmarking, and strategic planning tools. He has a bachelors degree in accounting from Bryant College and an MBA in finance from Pace University. His professional affiliations include American Production and Inventory Control Society, National Association of Purchasing Managers, Institute of Management Accountants, and American Society for Quality Control.

RICHARD D. JONES is director of quality, environment, and supply management (QES) for Honeywell's MICRO SWITCH Division in Freeport, Illinois. A graduate of the

Ohio Institute of Technology, he received his bachelors degree in marketing from Temple University and a masters degree in international management from the American Graduate School of International Management– Thunderbird, Arizona. As director of QES, he is responsible for leading the division's total quality management councils.

RODGER S. KLINE has been with Acxiom Corporation since 1973. He serves as the corporate leader and champion for financial results, business planning, activity-based management, economic value added implementation and compensation systems. He graduated from the University of Arkansas and holds a degree in electrical engineering.

JOHN SHIELY is president and chief operating officer of Briggs & Stratton Corporation and director of the Wisconsin chapter of the Association for Corporate Growth. He holds a masters degree in management from the Kellogg Graduate School of Management at Northwestern University and a law degree from Marquette University.

ROBERT STASEY is director of quality improvement at Analog Devices, Inc. A frequent industry speaker, he is an authority on total quality management assessment, policy deployment, and implementation of the necessary infrastructure to transform company culture toward the practice of continuous improvement. His book, *Crossroads,*

describes a four-year journey toward world-class
excellence through TQM and employee involvement.
He earned a bachelors degree from Indiana University
and an MBA from Depaul University.

PAUL THERRIEN is operations controller of Alpha
Industries, Inc., in Woburn, Massachusetts, and an instruc-
tor in cost accounting at Middlesex College. He has exten-
sive experience in designing accounting and management
control processes and speaks frequently on management
accounting topics. He received his bachelors degree in
accounting from Merrimack College and holds an MBA
from Rivier College.

GLENN UMINGER has 20 years experience in management accounting and production systems in manufacturing organizations, 10 of which are with Toyota Motor
Manufacturing, North America where he established
the management accounting function. He was recently
appointed manager in production control at the start-up
phase of the newly established manufacturing headquar-
ters of Toyota. He received his bachelors degree in
accounting from the University of Kentucky and holds
an MBA from Xavier University.